THE BATTLE FOR

ABERDEEN

1644

THE BATTLE FOR
ABERDEEN
1644

Chris Brown

TEMPUS

First published 2002

PUBLISHED IN THE UNITED KINGDOM BY:

Tempus Publishing Ltd
The Mill, Brimscombe Port
Stroud, Gloucestershire GL5 2QG
www.tempus–publishing.com

PUBLISHED IN THE UNITED STATES OF AMERICA BY:

Tempus Publishing Inc.
2 Cumberland Street
Charleston, SC 29401
(Tel: 1-888-313-2665)
www.tempuspublishing.com

British Library Cataloguing in Publication Data.
A catalogue record for this book is available from the British Library.

ISBN 0 7524 2340 1

Typesetting and origination by Tempus Publishing.
PRINTED AND BOUND IN GREAT BRITAIN.

CONTENTS

ACKNOWLEDGEMENTS

The list of friends, relatives and acquaintances who have in so many ways helped me with this book is, as ever, far too extensive to include in its entirety. However, certain individuals and groups simply must be mentioned: Billy Wright of the re-enactment group 'Frasers Dragoons' based in Aberdeenshire were kind enough to invite me to attend an event which was not open to the public so that I could take many of the photographs which appear in this book, and provide me with a wealth of information about the practicalities of war on foot in seventeenth-century Scotland; Francine Plimpton, Rob Hill, and Sue Dudley of 'Sir William Waller's Lifeguard of Horse' provided me with pictures and information concerning mounted warfare. My parents, Peter and Margaret Brown, supplied pictures of Aberdeen and some sound historical criticism. The local studies unit of Midlothian Public Libraries has again proved to be a tower of strength, and I am indebted to my son Robert for rescuing me from computer problems. Above all others I am beholden to my wife, Pat, who has had to put up with my endless meanderings as well as driving me from Penicuik to Aberdeen and back again on a particularly unpleasant day so that I could spend an hour taking photographs.

As yet I have discovered no way of making other people responsible for my mistakes; therefore I must accept any and all faults as my own.

1

THE ROOTS OF THE WAR OF
THE THREE KINGDOMS, 1637–42

On 1 September 1644, a few miles from the town of Perth, James Graham, Earl of Montrose won what would be the first in a series of battles that would make him one of Scotland's most famous generals. Montrose had returned to Scotland to further the cause of King Charles I against the Scottish government, but as recently as 1640 he had led a Scottish army into England in defiance of the King. As a devout Presbyterian his religious principles conflicted with the designs of the King and led him to add his signature to the Covenant of 1638, but his support for the rights and privileges of the Crown in civil matters brought him into conflict with his political allies among the Covenanting movement.

If Montrose had not defected to the King, the Royalist cause in Scotland would never have come to anything, but why was there such strong and widespread opposition to the King in the first place? How did Charles I come to lose the support of his northern kingdom to the extent that the Scottish government should go to war with its King, not once, but three times in the space of five years?

The Union of Crowns in 1603 had brought Scotland and England under the same monarch, James VI, but they still remained separate countries in

1. Henry VIII by Hans Holbein.

every sense – different parliaments, different taxes, different laws and, crucially, different forms of Protestant Christianity. Inevitably, James' accession to the throne of England greatly reduced the amount of time that he could devote to governing Scotland. Yet the stability of the administration that he had built up over the preceding twenty years and his astute management of the different interest groups that comprised the political society of early seventeenth-century Scotland allowed his government to flourish despite the fact that he spent almost all of the rest of his life in England. In theory James believed that as King he was answerable only to God for his conduct, but in practice he was generally more interested in pragmatic compromise than principled conflict. Charles saw things rather differently. Like his father he favoured a closer relationship between the two kingdoms, and in particular he favoured conformity of Church government and religious practice. Both England and Scotland were overwhelmingly Protestant, but the nature of reformation in each country was radically different. In England the departure from Roman Catholicism was the result of Henry VIII falling out with the Pope over whether or not he could get a divorce from Catherine of Aragon in order to marry his mistress Anne Boleyn. In Scotland the Reformation was a social and political revolution. Effectively the existing secular aspects of the Church in England became the Church *of* England – essentially replacing Roman Catholicism with Anglo-Catholicism. The actual doctrine and liturgy of English churches changed very little, if at all, as a result of replacing the Pope with the monarch as head of the Church. In Scotland the Reformation changed the entire nature of the Church as an institution; it stopped being Catholic in nature and became increasingly Calvinist Presbyterian. The first priority of the reformers was to renew the pastoral aspect of the Kirk, which had fallen into deep decay. In order to supervise the parish clergy a number of regional 'superintendents' were appointed. For all practical intents and purposes the superintendents inherited the ecclesiastical authority of the bishops, but the authority of the Pope was not so readily displaced by that of the King.

The fervour with which the new form of Kirk practice was accepted varied across the country, but broadly speaking the Reformation of 1560 was acceptable to the majority of Scots at all levels of society. Throughout his personal reign, James VI had made a number of almost counter-reformatory changes to the Kirk, particularly in regard to the position of bishops through the Kirk settlement of 1610, but he always managed to make these changes without alienating public opinion enough to affect support for the Crown.

Charles inherited two crowns from his father, but not the political acumen required to keep his authority secure in either realm. Armed with his own conception of the divine right of kings and believing that the Royal

Prerogative was a suitable instrument of government he took no heed of opposition to his plans for the effective 'anglicanisation' of the Scottish Church. As Charles was the head of the Church in England, he saw no reason why he should be only a member, however exalted and influential, of the Church in Scotland, so he took steps to achieve an effective and recognised primacy. When the Scots made their opposition to his plans clear through the promotion of the 'National Covenant' in 1638, Charles was not prepared to negotiate with the signatories, let alone accept their demands for the security of the Presbyterian form of worship and Church government, so he set about raising an army to coerce their acceptance of his authority. The Covenant in its original form had been framed with great care to avoid infringement of the Royal Prerogative, but it was still far too radical for Charles. No doubt he felt that he would be able to overawe the Scots with military might; England was after all a much wealthier country with a much larger population. Unfortunately for Charles there was precious little English public interest in fighting the Scots. By May 1639 the King had mustered an army of sorts at Berwick, but he lacked the experienced officers that would have been required to adequately train and lead it.

There was only one military action of any note during this campaign. A force of 3,000 (mostly if not entirely cavalry) was dispatched across the border under Lord Holland to seize the town of Kelso, only to be repulsed by a

2. Brawl in St Giles, Edinburgh, on the introduction of the new service book, 23 July 1637.

3. Engraving of Charles I.

4. Portrait of James VI of Scotland and I of England and Anna of Denmark.

5. The Solemn League and Covenant accepted by Parliament and imposed on the people of Scotland, England and Ireland, in 1643, from a contemporary pamphlet.

brigade of about 1,200 Scottish infantry under General Robert Munro, who drove off the English troops with little difficulty. The effect on morale of this action must have been severe for the King's army. If his cavalry could make no headway against an inferior force of infantry what hope was there for an ill-motivated army faced by a larger and more enthusiastic force of Scots under the command of experienced professional officers? Fortunately for Charles, the Scots were prepared to negotiate rather than force a battle on the King despite his exceptional vulnerability.

The humiliation for Charles was immense. He had no choice but to accede to the demands of the Scots – chiefly that the King should not interfere in the business of the Kirk. Part of the problem in recruiting and maintaining an army to fight the 'Bishop's War' of 1639 had been Charles' financial position. Even if he had been able to recruit an army large enough to face the Scots with any prospect of success he would not have been able to find the money to pay for their equipment, let alone their wages. Nonetheless, undaunted by his failure to defeat the Scots in 1639, he made a second attempt in 1640.

In order to fund this expedition he had to summon what would become known as the 'Short Parliament'. It was short because it was not prepared to sanction raising taxation to fight the Scots on an issue of limited significance to English affairs and instead demanded that internal matters be considered first, so Charles prorogued Parliament. He had temporarily removed a focus for the discontented, but he had done nothing to further his own cause. The campaign of 1640 did Charles no good and a great deal of harm. The Scottish government, completely dominated by Covenanters, had no Royalist party to speak of. The men who had attended Charles' English Parliament had been humiliated by his high-handedness in dismissing them without addressing their grievances and he had lost any military credibility by provoking a second 'Bishops' War', which he had lost almost as soon as it had begun.

On 20 August 1640 the Scottish army crossed the border. Among the senior officers was one James Graham, Marquis of Montrose, who would one day be the King's Lieutenant in Scotland and who would win a string of victories against the Scottish Parliamentarians. The Scottish army had crossed the border, by-passed Berwick, engaged an English army at Newburn, routed it in an almost bloodless action and advanced to Newcastle, which surrendered immediately. The King's prestige was certainly at a low ebb, and it sank lower yet. The occupation of Newcastle gave the Scots control over the northern English coal industry. Since London was dependent on coals from Newcastle for winter fuel the King's popularity in his English capital would be further damaged if the Scots cut off the supply of coal. As if that were not bad enough, the Scots demanded a payment of £850 per day to maintain their occupation army. This extra burden on top of the costs of a failed campaign forced the King to call another Parliament in England in the hope

Left 6. Replacing shoes and hose (woollen socks) was a perennial problem for Civil War soldiers.
Middle 7. Long boots were in great demand for protection against the wet, but were too expensive for most soldiers.
Right 8. Fanciful as it might seem a boot can make a surprisingly practical holster.

9. James Graham, first Marquis of Montrose.

of getting approval for taxation that he had been denied by the 'Short Parliament'. The Scottish Parliament was already completely beyond the King's control. In June 1640 it had convened without the consent, let alone the instruction, of the King. It had been the practice of Charles, and of his father, to appoint a commissioner to the Scottish Parliament to represent the King and to safeguard the royal interest. However Parliament now elected its own president and asserted its right to do so without consulting the King at all – another serious blow to royal authority.

Unable to further his policies and interests in Scotland through the customary practices of patronage and pressure, and unable to pay for his last campaign against the Scots, let alone find the funds to start a new one, Charles was forced to summon the Parliament of England (the 'Long Parliament') in the hope of getting a grant of taxation, which would allow him to raise an army that would be a match for his opponents in the northern kingdom. Left to his own devices Charles might not have summoned his English Parliament and would have sought to raise money through other means, but for the insis-

10. and 11. Commanders of the Covenanting wars: Archibald Campbell, 8th Earl of Argyll, (left) and Alexander Leslie (right).

12. Buff coats were in great demand for both horse and foot soldiers to offer some protection from the rain as much as from sword cuts.

tence of the Scottish government, whose military dominance effectively brooked no argument.

The members of the English Parliament were by no means universally opposed to the idea of a war against the Scots, but they had an agenda of their own to pursue. Charles had summoned no Parliament in England for eleven years before the 'Short Parliament' of April 1640, which he dismissed after less than a month when he had not found it to be sufficiently pliable. The new Parliament was determined to ensure that its own issues would be dealt with satisfactorily before it would consider the King's financial difficulties in general and his Scottish problems in particular, which were after all, almost completely of his own making.

By summoning Parliament, the King had added to his problems in England without making any contribution to solving his problems in Scotland. Charles' behaviour tended to alienate moderates, and his willingness to sacrifice his supporters for illusory short-term gains with his enemies did not help him to keep his friends. As the new Parliament continued to press the King, he was continually forced to make concessions that inevitably further undermined his authority and prestige, thus encouraging his opponents to press for greater power. No doubt Charles saw the appeasement of opposition in the Parliament of England as a temporary expedient; a means of securing the financial measures necessary to pursue his policies in Scotland. Once he had settled matters in Scotland to his liking he would be able to concentrate properly on his English problems.

The English Parliament was largely a conservative body of prosperous gentlemen, not a gathering of revolutionaries; the last thing anybody wanted was a civil war, but they did hope to effect a number of permanent changes in the system of government. These changes were hardly radical, let alone revolutionary, but they were still more than Charles could readily accept. The political struggle in Parliament between the supporters of the King and his opponents did not necessarily have to develop into a war, but the intransigent ideology of the King and, increasingly, of his opponents, made it harder and harder to avoid.

The King's attempt to dismiss Parliament and the refusal of Parliament to be dismissed brought matters to a head. Eventually, in August 1642 the King left London for Nottingham, where he started to raise another army, not for war with the Scots, this time, but for war in England. Parliamentary opposition to the King did not automatically mean military opposition. Many MPs, such as Edward Hyde, who had been quite vociferous in their opposition to Charles' policies and demands, could not bring themselves to side with his enemies in war. The same is true of those who did not share Charles' religious beliefs. Sir Edmund Verney, one of the foremost puritans in England, would

13. A thick, lined coat was vital for keeping out the cold, but soon
became heavy and cumbersome in the rain.

be killed in action at the battle of Edgehill, carrying Charles' personal banner and another prominent puritan, Sir Ralph Hopton, would be one of the most consistently competent generals in the Royalist cause although he had been a firm political opponent of Charles' arbitrary conduct of government before the war.

The period of conflicts traditionally known as 'The English Civil War' is increasingly seen as one of the wave of 'wars of religion' that erupted intermittently throughout Europe in the sixteenth and seventeenth centuries. There was certainly a religious element to each of these conflicts, but they were not the product of religious issues alone. In Scotland the war was just as much to do with curtailing the Royal Prerogative and Crown patronage as the means of ecclesiastical government as it was to do with any question of doctrine or liturgy. An important aspect of the religious conflict was the support of the King for an episcopalian system of Church government in spite of the widespread hostility to bishops throughout most of the country. The chief law officer of Scotland, the Lord Advocate Sir Thomas Hope, had even ruled that the office of bishop had no status in the Scottish Church or government. This ruling was of course directly contrary to the policies of the King and therefore another challenge to Charles' personal prestige as well as his regal authority.

The support of the King for the privileges and power of the bishops was a matter of considerable political significance. Since the appointment of bishops was in the King's gift the very existence of the episcopacy gave the King the opportunity to appoint men that he could rely on, men who would be in his debt, to positions of considerable power and influence. The abolition of episcopacy in Scotland had been a product of the Reformation, but James VI had managed to procure a grudging acceptance of the appointment of four bishops in 1600. These men did not enjoy the same status or range of powers as their equivalents in England but bishops sat in the Scottish Parliament as well as the English one, thereby potentially providing the nucleus of a Crown party in Scottish politics. The failure of the King or his representative Hamilton to encourage the development of such a party was obviously instrumental in the collapse of Charles' power in Scotland in the late 1630s. With no real platform of support in any part of the community, the King's participation in Scottish politics degenerated into a series of belated concessions to his opponents, which did nothing to further his authority.

In practice, by the autumn of 1641 the King had little to offer the Scots that they had not already taken for themselves. The Scots had effectively established a degree of political and religious independence that Charles could not hope to defeat as long as he faced concerted opposition in England. The English Parliament on the other hand could offer the Scots attractive economic benefits if they continued their resistance to the King. Not only were the majority of the remaining Parliamentarians in London broadly sympathetic to the religious policies of the Scottish government, but they were also in a position to make attractive concessions to the Scots on issues of trade. The King was hardly in a position to compete with the economic favour that Parliament could extend to an ally as long as the biggest market and concentration of capital in either country, London, was outside royal control. Charles had in any case already lost most of what little support he had enjoyed in the Scottish Parliament due to his high-handed behaviour, particularly, though not exclusively, in religious matters.

The eventual alliance of the Scots and the English Parliamentarians was not inevitable, but the policies of the King throughout his reign encouraged his opponents to make common cause against him. The practical result of that alliance from the point of view of the English Parliamentarians was the deployment of a Scottish army against the King's forces in the north of England. Not only did this deployment obviously require a local strategic and tactical response from the King at a time when he had more than enough for his troops to deal with already, it released Parliamentary troops for service in other areas and allowed a rationalisation and concentration of anti-monarchical military effort.

14. Targes (round shields) were carried by many Highland troops and possibly by some Irish soldiers.

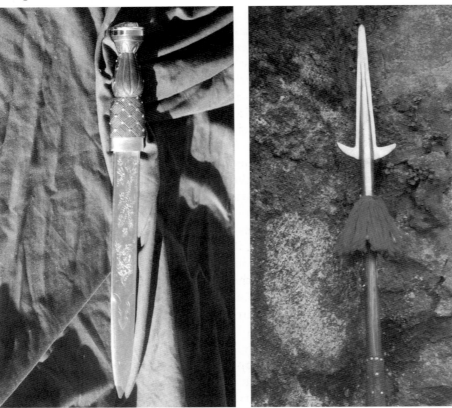

Left 15. The peculiarly Scottish form of dagger known as a dirk [dirk supplied by 'Battle Orders' Surrey].
Right 16. Other than pikes, polearms like this partisan were very much a badge of office
for senior NCOs.

The King could not, of course, afford to ignore his northern kingdom. Regardless of whether the Scots sided with his English enemies, preservation of his kingly prestige demanded that he take action. For years the King had depended on the Marquis (later the Duke) of Hamilton to protect his interests in Scotland, but Hamilton was a poor tool for the purpose. He was seldom inclined to relate a true picture of the state of the King's affairs, preferring to present his master with unreasonably optimistic impressions of events north of the border. Hamilton himself was hardly a popular figure in Scotland; his own mother, Anna Cunningham, had raised and trained a troop of horse for the Scottish government during the 'Bishop's War' and had publicly declared her willingness to shoot her son with her own hand should the opportunity arise.

The outbreak of the Irish rebellion of the Confederacy in 1641 brought the issues of war-taxation and control of the army sharply into focus, and the possibility of civil war in England could no longer be ignored. The Royalist victory at the first engagement, Edgehill, on 23 October 1642 proved to be typical of the early part of the war; a pattern of marginal victories which often had little discernible effect on the war generally. Despite extreme financial difficulties and poorer recruitment the King's armies enjoyed a considerable degree of success until 1644. The arrival of the Scottish army in England tipped the military balance toward the Parliamentarians and Charles had insufficient resources to restore the situation. Hamilton had lost the King's favour – indeed when he arrived at Oxford (the Royalist capital) in December 1643 to apprise the King of events in Scotland he was promptly arrested for failing to fulfil Charles' hopes and expectations.

Charles realised that he had to do something to remove the Scots from the main theatre of operations, and he was convinced that the best course of action would be to inaugurate a war on Scottish soil that would force the Edinburgh government to recall their troops from England. Hamilton was self-evidently not fit for the task. Even if he had been able to retain the King's confidence, he had a poor reputation in Scotland and would find it difficult, if not impossible, to raise troops. All the same, Charles had to do something to change the course of the war. He had been able to stabilise the war situation in Ireland by procuring an armistice with the Irish Confederacy. The terms of this arrangement – known as 'The Cessation' – removed one of the King's burdens immediately insofar as he could concentrate on his English problems, but it also provided an opportunity to do something about his Scottish difficulties. When the actions of the Covenanting Scottish government had started to become a real challenge in the late 1630s, Charles had planned to make war against them by mounting an enormously complicated series of simultaneous operations; the main approach by a large army from England would be supported by a sea-borne force, which would conduct

17. A musketeer filling the individual powder charges on his bandolier. The term 'apostles' did not come into vogue until the nineteenth century.

operations against the east coast of Scotland and two separate descents on the west coast by troops from Ireland. The entire operation was a disastrous failure – the fleet only made one landing and achieved nothing of any value and the proposed force from Ireland fared no better, but the deteriorating position of the Royalist cause in 1644 called for a new initiative and the King once again looked to Ireland for troops.

The 'Cessation agreement' was developed into an alliance, and the Irish Confederacy was prepared to allow the enlistment of Irish troops for a new campaign in Scotland. With Hamilton in disgrace the King needed a new champion for his cause in Scotland. Of all the Scottish Royalist sympathisers, the man with the greatest potential for raising an army was the Earl of Huntly, but he was seen – not unreasonably – as being less than wholehearted in his commitment to almost anything. Although he was a convinced and devout episcopalian his efforts for the King in the past had been less than spectacularly successful and the King had to look elsewhere for a Scottish leader. His choice fell on James Graham, Earl, and later Marquis, of Montrose.

This was not a move that would endear the King to Huntly; Huntly was a more senior member of the Scottish aristocracy than Montrose, so the King's appointment reflected badly on Huntly's prestige and as if that was not bad

Left 18. Other than the widely worn blue bonnet, there was nothing to particularly distinguish the majority of Scottish troops from soldiers throughout Europe.
Right 19. Although most infantry wore grey coats and breeches, a few wore red coats like this one.

enough, in the days when Montrose had been a prominent and dedicated supporter of the Covenanting government he had, unwittingly, been instrumental in having Huntly arrested and imprisoned to prevent him organising opposition to the new style of government that had come into being as a result of the political and religious opposition to the Crown.

Montrose was not particularly popular among the King's advisors. He was seen as a man who would promise a lot but deliver little or nothing to the Royalist cause. Some degree of hostility was almost inevitable given the central role that Montrose had played in the 'Covenanter Revolution' of the late 1630s that had effectively removed power from the hands of the King. Montrose was not always the easiest person to get on with. He was extremely prickly about questions of his honour and status, he did, however, have a number of sterling qualities, he was a staunch monarchist, a man of action and personally courageous to a fault. In any case, by 1644 Charles' Scottish supporters were rather thin on the ground, and he could not afford to be too choosy about who would represent the King's authority in Scotland given that the leaders of Scottish society were almost without exception supporters of the government. Montrose himself had been a leading light in the Covenanting movement during the late 1630s and early 1640s. He had been

20. This man could just as easily be a member of an Irish regiment as a Scottish one.

among the first signatories of the 'National Covenant' and had been one of the commanders of the army that had humiliated the King in the 'Bishop's War'. Montrose defected to the King when he came to believe that the government set up by the Covenanting movement had encroached too much on royal authority. Throughout the development of the conflict between the King and the Covenanters Montrose had kept in touch with the King, declaring himself to be loyal to the monarchy in keeping with the sentiments expressed in the wording of the original Covenant. In his view, it was the other leaders of the Covenanting movement who had abandoned their duty to their King in their zeal for protecting the position of the established Kirk. Unsurprisingly, those other leaders saw matters differently. Montrose's continued communications with the King and his involvement in various 'bands' aimed at restoring the King's authority within the framework of Scottish political and religious traditions destroyed his credibility among his erstwhile colleagues and drove him back into the King's faith. By June 1641 his actions had aroused enough opposition that his political enemies were able to have him arrested and imprisoned in Edinburgh Castle to await trial for treason. Charles, in Edinburgh to attend Parliament, was not easily persuaded to intervene to save Montrose because he was intent on appeasing the government, but did eventually procure his release just before returning to England. Montrose had been instrumental in bringing the King's problems in Scotland to a head, but imprisonment proved his loyalty, and his willingness to serve his King was never in question thereafter. In January 1644 Montrose was appointed the King's Lieutenant-general in Scotland, and a fortnight later promotion to Lieutenant-governor with authority over all the King's subjects – always supposing he could find a way to impose that authority.

A combined effort on the part of the King's supporters in Scotland took place in April of 1644. Huntly declared for the King and seized Aberdeen, capturing stocks of arms and ammunition, but he could raise little more than 1,000 men and a large government force under the Marquis of Argyll suppressed Huntly's rebellion and administered a sharp demonstration of 'fire and the sword' throughout the north-east to discourage support for the Royalists in the future. Huntly's rising was not helped by the fact that his son and heir, Lord Gordon, was on the other side, thus dividing the resources of the house.

At the same time, Montrose led a modest force of infantry and cavalry from Carlisle into Dumfriesshire. Before he could achieve very much he lost the majority of his force through mutiny. Assurances of support from various quarters failed to materialise, and the approach of a regiment of government infantry forced Montrose to beat a hasty retreat to Carlisle.

Receiving temporary command of a force of 2,000 infantry and 500 cavalry under the Marquis of Newcastle, Montrose conducted operations against the Scottish troops under General Leslie, who had been stationed in the north of England under the terms of the alliance between the Scottish and English Parliaments. This campaign was prospering and showing Montrose in a good light until events elsewhere demanded an urgent re-allocation of Royalist resources. On 2 July the armies of the two Parliaments had secured a major victory over the King's army at Marston Moor. Montrose met with the defeated Royalist commander, Prince Rupert at Richmond the day after the battle and promptly had his command removed.

Without troops at his disposal what he could achieve for his King was open to question. There was no Royalist force under arms in Scotland and no apparent likelihood of a spontaneous rising, any Royalist effort in the northern kingdom would have to originate elsewhere. So he covertly crossed the border with two comrades, Colonel William Sibbald and Sir William Rollo to try to inaugurate nothing less than a Royalist counter-revolution. However romantic

21. Prince Rupert (1619–82). Royalist cavalry officer, appointed
General of the horse by Charles I.

he may have been, and however enthusiastic for his master's cause, Montrose was an intelligent man, and he must have had confidence that appeals for support in a war against the government would not go unheeded and that the venture was not a lost cause. When Montrose slipped across the border and headed toward Perthshire he was not merely optimistic of enlisting help, he was looking for a force that was already in existence.

2

AUGUST 1644

King Charles could spare nothing from his English armies and had to look towards his new Irish allies to provide the manpower for his next venture. The Confederacy allowed troops to be raised in Ireland for the King's cause, and they were dispatched to the west coast of Scotland where they captured Mingarry and Lochaline Castles. No doubt it was thought that these minor strongholds would provide depot facilities for the import of recruits and supplies from Ireland, but the ships on which such re-supply would depend were soon captured by government forces, so the Irish brigade was effectively stranded in Scotland. In the hope of raising further men for the King's army in Scotland, the commander of the brigade, Alistair MacDonald, led his force west toward Atholl. His reception was hardly an overwhelming endorsement of the King's cause. Many of the people that Alistair looked to for support were unwilling to commit themselves to so precarious a venture, many refused to have anything to do with a force of mercenaries, foreign by both nationality and religion. He did manage to raise about 500 men by the simple, if drastic, expedient of sending out parties to arrest local landholders, having them brought to his camp, showing them the King's commission and demanding that they call out their tenants and dependants – largely MacPhersons – to fight for the King.

22. The battlefield of Tippermuir, a few miles west of Perth. This was the first of the remarkable series of Royalist victories throughout 1644–45.

The King's Lieutenant, Montrose, was in Methven Forest in Perthshire, without troops or money and in danger of being apprehended by government forces when Alistair's communication reached him. Montrose immediately set out for Atholl to *rendezvous* with the Irish troops at Blair Atholl on the 29 August 1644. The government had, of course, taken steps to counter the Irish force and instructions had been given to enlist Atholl men for emergency army service. Tradition has it that they and the Irish regiments were on the verge of combat when Montrose arrived on the scene, showed his commission from the King and immediately received the support of the local forces. This seems just a little too good to be true. As Stuart Reid (*The Campaigns of Montrose*) has pointed out the further defection of 500 Lowland men from the government to the Royalists at nearby Buchanty the next day certainly suggests some degree of collusion.

Between the Irish troops, the few hundred MacPhersons and the 500 Lowland 'defectors' Montrose now commanded an army of something approaching 3,000 infantry, half of them Irish professionals, the remainder locally enlisted men with little or no training and short of arms. There was no cavalry to protect his column on the march or to conduct *reconnaissance* and no artillery.

What was Montrose to do with this force? If he was to keep it in existence at all he had to arrange for food and ammunition, both of which were in short

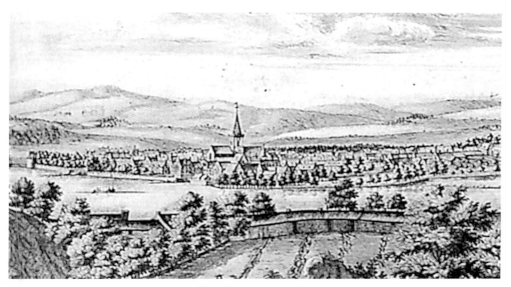

23. Perth in the seventeenth century.

supply. If he was to retain the confidence and goodwill of the Irish troops he would need to be able to offer them at least the prospect of rewards worthy of the risks they were undertaking. The money that would be required to keep the army in the field could only come from Scottish resources; the King had so many pressing problems already that there was no real prospect of a steady supply of funds from Oxford, the Royalist capital in England. Montrose needed to capture a town. Perth was the nearest town of any size, and Montrose would have been obliged to at least attempt its capture in order to demand money and materiel from the community. But there was another reason: the government had started to make moves against the Royalist insurgents and had already ordered a muster of troops at Perth.

With one army operating in England and another in Ireland totalling something in the region of 30,000 men between them, it is hardly surprising that there were few experienced officers and men available to the government.

As the Royalists approached Perth from the west the commander of the government force at Perth, Lord Elcho, drew his troops out of the town to meet with Montrose at Tippermuir. Sources sympathetic to the Royalists claim that the government army was about 6,000 strong, but it seems likely that in fact it was about half that number that faced the Royalists on 1 September 1644. Certainly it was a more conventional army by the standards of the time, comprising horse, as well as foot, and even a small quantity of light artillery, but a scratch force of conscripts suddenly called together was unlikely to be a match for the trained Irish regiments.

The fighting at Tippermuir was brief and was followed by a pursuit that took the Royalists all the way to Perth. The defeat of the government army precluded any attempt to deny the town to Montrose, and he was happy to accept its surrender.

Victory allowed Montrose to feed and clothe his army at the expense of his enemy and undoubtedly procured him a useful quantity of arms and ammunition, but it did not bring him very much in the way of recruits. Worse than that, he could not hold his army together. The Highland troops slipped away in large numbers, but the government was already mustering a new army at Stirling under the Marquis of Argyll and the Earl of Lothian less than a week after Tippermuir. With no real local enthusiasm for the Royalist cause Montrose could not hope to hold Perth as a centre of operations so he decided to make his way northwards in search of recruits. First he marched east to Dundee and demanded the surrender of the town to Crown authority. Whether or not Montrose expected anything to come of such a demand he had to make it. The King's representative could hardly pass by such an important town without making some gesture of authority. The burgesses were not impressed however, and Montrose did not have enough of an army to enforce his will.

Argyll's army to the south was daily growing in strength, and not just in emergency conscripts. Regular regiments were being recalled from service in England with a view to putting down the Royalist insurrection in very short order. If that insurrection was to have any chance of success Montrose needed to have more men and to feed the ones he already had; the way south was barred to him by Argyll and the River Forth, so he marched north toward Aberdeen.

3

SCOTTISH ARMIES IN THE 1640s

THE INFANTRY

The army of Montrose has been the subject of a good deal of debate, particularly in connection with the Highland contingent and their approach to combat. The battle of Aberdeen, however, was fought without any significant contribution from Scottish infantry on the Royalist side, either Highland or Lowland. Almost all of the 1,500 or so infantry under the command of Montrose on the 13 September 1644 were in the ranks of the three Irish regiments. These were conventionally armed soldiers, who would have been just as much 'at home' in the army of any northern European country as they were in Scotland. They do seem to have been relatively short of pikemen compared to musketeers, but the optimum proportion of pike to shot was a matter of some professional debate. The armies of both King and Parliament in England favoured two muskets for every pike as a general principle, but this was by no means universal. Scottish regiments operating in England seem to have had a slightly larger proportion of pikes, perhaps two for every three

24. Colour bearer from a government regiment. Each company in the regiment would have one colour.

25. Government colours were based on the Saltire, the national flag of Scotland. This one carries the legend 'for religion, country, crown and covenant'.

26. Musketeers loading. A well-trained soldier could fire three times in a minute, but would soon run out of ammunition.

27. A matchlock musket. The steel curl visible above the trigger mechanism held a length of smouldering matchcord. When the trigger was pulled, the matchcord would be brought into contact with powder in a pan on the right-hand side of the musket. That powder would be ignited and then in turn ignite the charge in the breech of the musket.

musketeers. This may have been a product of the Scottish army having a much smaller cavalry component, which would force the infantry regiments to be more self-reliant against enemy cavalry than would be the case in English armies.

The musket, then, was the primary weapon of the majority of the infantry and the firefight was the crucial element in deciding victory in battle. The battlefield role of artillery, such as it was, was to cause disorder in the ranks of the enemy infantry. The tactical role of the cavalry was to disperse the enemy cavalry and then to deliver attacks on the flanks and rear of their infantry once the main battle had been joined.

The seventeenth-century musket was a heavy, unreliable and inaccurate weapon which required a complex drill for loading. It was not even particularly cheap, so why was it the weapon of the majority of soldiers? A bow was certainly more accurate in the hands of a trained practitioner, it had a much higher rate of 'fire', and the disappearance of body armour increased the potential lethality of the arrow. The advantage of the musket lay in the speed with which troops could be trained to use it. Proficient archery for military purposes required practice from an early age and was only really a practical proposition for men who were physically strong by nature. A man could be

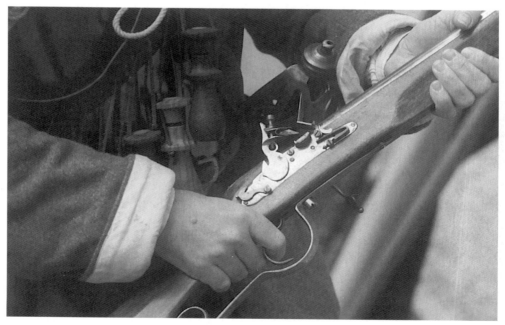

28. A flintlock musket or 'firelock'. This superseded the matchlock musket, and would remain in use with very little alteration until well into the nineteenth century.

29. Musketeer attaching a length of smouldering match to his musket.

30. Musketeer blowing on the end of his slow match to ensure that the ember at the end of the match is hot enough to ignite the powder charge when the match is applied at the firing pan of the musket.

31. Musket balls were carried in pockets or pouches.

32. Heavy broadswords were widely used, but officers and gentlemen were more inclined to carry rather finer examples of the swordsmith`s craft. [Sword supplied by 'Battle Orders', Surrey]

Left 33. Musketeer ramming powder and ball. In practice more experienced soldiers just tapped the butt of the musket in order to settle the powder charge.
Right 34. Soldiers on both sides had to make their own arrangements for their personal kit or provisions, such as this canvas roll.

trained to the musket in a matter of an hour or two, and it did not matter in the slightest whether the musketeer was big or small; as long as he could operate the trigger mechanism of the weapon he was capable of inflicting a lethal wound on any opponent. The weight of the round was such that almost any wound might be instantaneously fatal. Any wound in the torso, however it was inflicted, was very likely to become infected and bring about the death of the victim. An arm or leg wound from a musket ball was likely to do so much damage, particularly if the bone had been hit, that the only option for the surgeon was to perform an amputation. Wounds to limbs were of course just as likely to become infected and gangrenous as any other injuries, but wounds in the stomach area were almost invariably fatal due to the onset of peritonitis.

For decades musketeers had generally fought in much the same way regardless of what army they served in. The unit deployed for battle several ranks

35. Most troops were trained to fire in rotation; while the man in the front rank fires those in the subsequent ranks re-load their muskets. The man in the second rank is ready to step forward, aim and give fire as soon as the man in the front rank fires and retires.

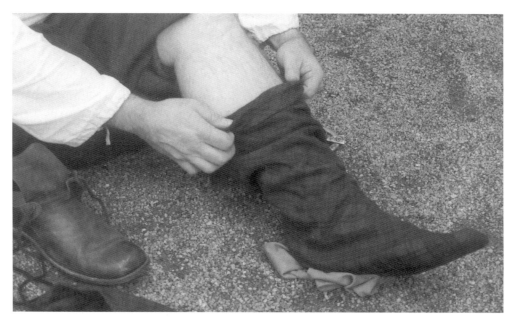

36. Diced hose, very fashionable among Highland men.

37. Powder horns were common but not universal. This musketeer carries a wooden powder box with an ingenius spout which measures the charge.

deep, ideally six or even eight, and each rank fired by rotation. The men in the front rank would fire and then make their way through their comrades to form a new rear rank and start the process of re-loading, while the rest of the unit shuffled forward to take their turn at shooting. The resulting fire was nearly continuous, but not especially effective. The muskets were not particularly well-made, the troops seldom received much in the way of 'live ammunition' training before combat, and the attraction of getting one's round off against the enemy and smartly making one's way to the rear rank is obvious. The fear and excitement generated by being in action, particularly for inexperienced and untrained troops would further impair the effectiveness of fire. The rotational method of fire had a number of disadvantages, but it continued to be the most common application of musket fire in battle because it was relatively easy to train the men to perform the drill adequately. For a man with little experience of fire-arms the complicated drill necessary to allow a reasonably consistent delivery of fire could be achieved more easily in a step-by-step manner in concert with his neighbours − if the man on either side of you is priming his musket, it is a fair bet that you should be priming yours.

The depth of the unit not only allowed a steady rolling fire on the enemy, it exposed less of the unit to enemy fire at any given moment and afforded at least an illusion of security to those loading their muskets. This rolling fire of the traditionally trained unit could only inflict a small number of casualties at each firing. If the unit comprised 300 musketeers in six ranks of fifty then a maximum of fifty casualties could be inflicted on the enemy at each firing. In practice only a tiny fraction of that figure would become casualties, even at very close range. The fire of such a unit must have been perceived by both the target and the firers themselves as being less dangerous than it seems to us. The fact that units could be persuaded to engage in lengthy firefights at all, let alone repeatedly, indicates that battle was not seen as a suicidal activity.

There was an alternative approach to the conduct of the firefight, and this may well have been the root of the remarkably consistent superiority of the Irish regiments over their Scottish opponents. A well-trained unit with confidence in its abilities and its leadership could forego the advantages of depth in favour of concentration of fire. The whole of the unit loading, aiming and firing as one simply put more rounds in the air at one command. Whether or not salvo firing was really more effective over the course of an extended firefight would not be important. As long as each man took much the same length of time to load and fire his musket, a similar quantity of rounds would be fired in a given period by two units of similar size; what mattered was the impression made on the participants on either side. A single volley of 300

38. Heavy basket hilted swords were the order of the day.

39. Carrying the pike. The weight of the pike and its awkwardness in even the lightest breeze made it very difficult to wield for all but the strongest men.

musket balls might well be enough to persuade troops firing in the more traditional method not to make a determined effort, whereas the sight of the enemy ranks being obviously depleted at each firing would be an encouragement to the firers. In an engagement between two bodies of experienced troops this difference in the concentration of fire may not have counted for much, but for the farmhands and artisans who found themselves enlisted in the fight against Montrose it might have been devastating.

Salvo firing demanded greater confidence in the unit because they would have to endure the enemy's fire more often, but on the other hand the men did not have to shuffle through the ranks of the unit and were thus more readily under the control of the officers and NCOs. The other advantage of salvo firing was that the unit could be deployed in three or four ranks if necessary without significantly reducing the effectiveness of fire in the early stages of the firefight. No more than three ranks could fire in one volley, so the usefulness of a fourth, fifth or sixth rank – although regiments apparently continued to form up that deep – was limited to providing replacements for men killed or wounded in the first three. The enemy's volleys would be delivered more often, but each volley from the salvo-trained unit would still be three times as effective.

Most of the infantry carried the musket, the remainder the pike. According to contemporary manuals pikes were to be 18 ft long, but in practice even the lightest breeze would make the weapon very difficult to handle for all but the very strongest men and, although it was strongly discouraged, soldiers tended to remove a couple of feet from the pike-shaft. Body armour seems to have been much less common among Scottish troops than English, but in both countries it was largely the preserve of pikemen. A fully equipped pikeman might have a helmet, breast-plate, back-plate, and tassets to protect his thighs. Worn in conjunction with a thick buff coat the wearer enjoyed a good deal of protection, and indeed encounters at 'push of pike' seem to have involved very few casualties. The *mêlée* presumably continued until one side or the other decided they had had enough and withdrew. As long as they withdrew in good order their opponents would be likely to follow up cautiously if at all, but a precipitate retreat would invite a pursuit and probably heavy losses. Both musketeers and pikemen were issued with swords in all the armies of the day. The tendency to dismiss the value of the sword in combat should not be accepted easily, however, for one thing, in the event of the disintegration of an enemy formation, pikemen would be hindered rather than helped by their primary weapon, and in any case, if the sword was useless, army administrators would have been more than happy not to spend money on them. Swords were quite expensive weapons, and remarkably fragile when abused. The notion that they would have been used primarily for chopping firewood does not bear examination, as a sword used for that purpose will soon break, and will never be anything like as effective as even a very small axe.

The normal deployment of an infantry regiment was into three bodies – two of musketeers and one of pikes. The pikemen stood in the centre of the regimental line and the musketeers on either side. The chief function of the pikemen was to protect the musketeers against cavalry, either on the march, where musketeers would be highly vulnerable to sudden attack, or in a general engagement where the enemy had already won the cavalry battle. The presence of the pikemen would allow the musketeers to keep up a fire against the cavalry from a position of relative safety. Frequently, especially when a commander was anxious about either the quantity or quality of his cavalry compared to the opposition, parties of musketeers would be deployed among the troops of cavalry. These parties, sometimes called 'commanded shot', would endeavour to cause disruption among the opposition and thereby provide opportunities for their own cavalry. This practice perhaps calls into question our perception of the pike. If the offensive capacity of the musketeer

40. A long wheel-lock horse pistol. Wheel locks and flintlocks meant that the user did not have to keep a length of matchcord smouldering in order to fire, but they were more expensive and less robust than the matchlock mechanism used on most muskets.

41. The wheel-lock horse pistol: the spring that powers the wheel which drives the flint against the steel to make a spark and ignite the charge needs to be 'wound up' with a small spanner.

Left 42. Typical cavalryman of the 1640s. Note the 'quilted' appearance of the saddle.
Right 43. A well-equipped horse soldier, with carbine and long pistol.

Left 44. Typical seventeenth-century cavalry.
Right 45. Few Civil War cavalrymen bore more armour than a 'pot' helmet and back and breast-plates. Note the pistol holsters at the front of the saddle.

was high enough to allow groups of them to operate as part of the cavalry battle, what was the function of the pike and why was it retained? Unlike the musket, the pike had the advantage of being waterproof. The incidence of misfires was high at the best of times, and even a light rain would reduce the efficiency of fire drastically. A unit armed only with muskets would be extremely vulnerable to attack from cavalry in wet weather. The musketeer elements of Civil War armies do not appear to have been very abundantly supplied with ammunition – not a problem for the pikemen. Although, the loading drill of the musket could be taught to most men in a reasonably short space of time, there would inevitably be some soldiers who would find the intricacies of firearms just too complex to get to grips with, so if they were big enough men to handle the pike, then pikemen they would be. A pike was considerably cheaper than a musket, and not very prone to damage even in the clumsiest hands. On top of all that, the pike was a traditional part of infantry armament, and the musketeers of the regiment would feel more secure in the company of their pikemen. Finally, while it is true that there are several examples of musket-armed troops holding their own against cavalry, either as part of the cavalry battle or in their own right, these men were probably drawn from the more competent and confident members of the army rather than the average rank and file.

THE CAVALRY

Although the cavalry component of both armies in Scotland was much smaller than in English armies, their contribution was often essential to success and just as significantly their failure to contribute was frequently a major contribution to failure. At Tippermuir Montrose had no cavalry at all, and the failure of Lord Elcho to exploit his advantage led to his defeat. At Aberdeen the effective commitment of the very tiny Royalist cavalry force would be a crucial element in achieving victory. A peculiarity of Scottish cavalry in the Civil War was the continued use of the lance. This is sometimes attributed to the poorer horses of Scottish cavalry units, though how the use of a lance would offset the difference in the quality of mounts is not clear. Other than the lance, Scottish cavalry carried much the same equipment as their counterparts elsewhere. Body armour was becoming less common among cavalry as well as pikemen. A well-equipped cavalry trooper would have a helmet, breast and back-plates, a steel 'bridle gauntlet' and very probably a buff coat, and a few wealthy gentlemen might aspire to being a 'cuirassier', with a closed-face helmet and leg armour, but these were few and

46. A well-equipped government cavalryman or dragoon.

47. Dragoons invariably fought dismounted. Although they were issued with swords they had neither the training nor the quality of horses required to deliver charges.

48. Civil War cavalry. Note the variety of equipment – no two riders are wearing quite the same pattern of helmet.

far between, possibly a reflection of the high cost of procuring and maintaining a suitable horse. To some extent the decreasing use of body armour throughout the sixteenth and seventeenth centuries was a reflection of improvements in fire-arms, but it was also a question of fashion. The lethality of a musket ball hurtling toward its target would not improve noticeably between 1640 and 1700, but body armour was almost completely abandoned in the same period.

For firepower the cavalry depended on the pistol and carbine. These were no more effective than the musket, but could at least be carried in pairs. Customarily, horsemen would try to fire their pistol with the muzzle actually in contact with an opposing cavalryman in the course of a *mêlée* – a comment on both the accuracy and the power of the weapon. If confronted by musketeers with no pike support, cavalry could attempt to charge 'home', sword in hand and scatter their enemy, probably inflicting heavy casualties. When faced with pikemen they could perform the manoeuvre known as the *caracole*. This called for the unit to advance in a rotation of ranks, each rank discharging their pistols at the enemy, retiring to re-load and repeating the process until the engagement was decided. The *caracole* is widely seen by historians as being an impractical evolution, but we should bear in mind that as it was a normal practice of cavalry units throughout Europe, it is unreasonable to assume that seventeenth-century commanders would not have retained the method if it

49. Oliver Cromwell.

Left 50. Tending the horse before the man. The ubiquitous nature of the equipment – buff coats and breastplates – made the cavalry of one army indistinguishable from the cavalry of another.
Right 51. Typical cavalryman of the Civil War, complete with pistols in saddle holsters and carbine slung behind.

did not procure results. Like the rotational approach to firing adopted by most infantry, the *caracole* required several ranks of men to produce a steady rolling fire sufficiently intense to intimidate the enemy.

The *caracole*, and the deep formation required to perform it effectively, was becoming less popular by the 1640s. Increasingly the cavalry was being deployed three ranks deep and were being trained to carry their attack right into the ranks of the enemy using the sword as the primary weapon and the pistol as a secondary weapon if a static *mêlée* should develop or against formed infantry. The new practice of charging 'home' called for an advance at greater speed and in closer order than had been the practice in the past. This should not be taken to mean a headlong dash toward the enemy, but rather a controlled trot, or at best a canter, which would allow the unit to cover the ground at a reasonable pace but still be slow enough to allow the worst-mounted men in the unit to keep up with the best and, just as impor-

52. Although all of the cavalrymen in this picture are 'typical' of the period, no two of them carry the same kit.

tantly, to enable commanders to keep their units under control. The 'dressing' of cavalry units – the intervals between ranks and files – has been the subject of some debate. The traditional picture of cavalry charging 'knee-to-knee' probably needs to be taken less than literally for the majority of mounted units.

In a well-trained unit with well-trained horses it was probably practical to maintain the formation of the unit adequately at the trot, with only an interval of less than half a metre between troopers in the same rank and with an interval of perhaps two metres between ranks as an absolute minimum. Even the two-metre gap between ranks would have been very risky for movement under fire. A horse that fell or reared would almost inevitably cause problems for at least one horse and rider in the following rank.

Government cavalry raised for home service seem to have mostly relied on the deeper formation, whereas those regiments raised for service with the army in England seem to have adopted the three-rank formation by the time of Marston Moor, where David Leslie's cavalry brigade made a spirited attack, in support of Cromwell's units at the critical moment to turn that phase of the battle.

Although government cavalry regiments were organised in 'troops' of sixty or so men, the troop was an administrative rather than a tactical unit. In battle it was more common to divide the regiment into two squadrons, sometimes one with lances and one without. Cavalry units raised for home service rather

53. A cavalryman's pot helmet. Note the thick felt liner for comfort and protection from bruis-ing. Helmets like these were commonplace throughout Europe in the seventeenth century.

54. Back and breast-plates: although it is generally assumed that Scottish pikemen wore no armour, a contemporary source states clearly that a considerable quantity of armour was lost to the Royalists at the battle of Aberdeen.

than for the army in England seem mostly to have consisted of single troops with a strength of anything up to 100 men.

The majority of cavalry units were not all that well-trained, and even those units that started the war with good quality horses would soon find themselves requisitioning virtually any old nag with a leg at each corner due to the high attrition rate of horses on campaign. Horses can be remarkably frail creatures, and losses through natural causes would almost inevitably be greater than losses in action. Casualties on the battlefield were not usually very heavy. Units which are described in reports of actions as being completely destroyed more often than not turn up elsewhere within a short period of time, the implication being that the troops were scattered and consequently re-grouped rather than a replacement unit being raised.

Away from battle – and we should bear in mind that despite the fact that Montrose fought two battles in the space of a fortnight general engagements were really something of a rarity – the cavalry had to perform a variety of tasks. The most important of these functions were reconnaissance and foraging. The former was a task seldom carried out adequately in the Scottish Royalist army, which goes some way to explaining the regularity with which Montrose came close to being taken by surprise. To some extent this was a product of the superior numbers of cavalry available to the government forces, but it was also a reflection of a failure on the part of Montrose to maintain observation of the enemy. Foraging was, of course, carried out by the infantry as much as the cavalry, but a mounted unit could conduct search operations more easily and over a greater distance than men on foot could. The great problem in keeping a mounted force of any size under arms lay in the diffi-culty of securing sufficient quantities of foodstuffs on a regular basis. A horse that carries a soldier day-on-day cannot be expected to thrive on grass alone, even if it was to be allowed long periods for grazing. Even in the summer the cavalry would need to acquire large quantities of barley or oats to keep their mounts in reasonable condition. In the winter grazing would be less nutritious and the demand for grain would be that much heavier, so the passage of an army in wintertime would inevitably be a heavy burden on any community. Not only would grain stocks be confiscated – along with any useful-looking mounts – but the community would be faced with the prospect of having to slaughter or sell their remaining livestock or see the beasts starve.

Service in the cavalry had certain attractions compared to enlisting in the infantry. A cavalry soldier on the march might well walk as much as ride, but at least he rode some of the time, presumably enough of the time to make up for the chores and responsibilities of having a horse to look after. In battle the horse and man presented a bigger target than the soldier on shanks' pony, but if the action went badly the cavalryman was probably going to be able to make his escape more easily than the infantryman; if the action went well he might well be able to be in the forefront of looting the enemy camp.

The other horse-soldier common to Civil War armies was the dragoon. Essentially a mounted infantryman, the dragoon was in demand for the some of the tasks normally associated with the cavalry proper – *reconnaissance* and foraging – but also to provide mounted raiding parties with superior firepower to the pistols and carbines of the cavalry units. A typical task for a dragoon unit might be the capture of a specific objective ahead of the main body of the army, such as a bridge or ford. Dragoons fought on foot, with only one or two exceptions throughout the entire course of the war. Montrose never had the opportunity to develop a proper dragoon unit as such, but the government forces included at least one regiment (Frasers) and some government cavalry regiments included a company of dragoons as part of their establishment as well as the conventional troops of horse.

THE ARTILLERY

Although the government forces were quite well supplied with artillery, it had a fairly limited role on the battlefield. The common practice of the time was

55. The back and breast-plates were held in place by the straps over the shoulders and the leather strap around the waist.

to deploy the artillery immediately in front of the main line of battle or, if the terrain permitted, on higher ground behind that line. The battle of Aberdeen may have seen both formulae in use. The government artillery was stationed in front of the infantry but the Royalist guns were apparently positioned on rising ground near the Hardgate. Their fire was probably severely compromised by the general advance of the Royalist infantry, which occurred sometime after 11a.m.

The artillery train of any force inevitably trailed along at the tail of the column at a very slow pace indeed. In the event of an encounter with the enemy the guns might even be left out of the battle because of the time it would take to bring them into action. Lighter pieces were developed in an endeavour to provide the infantry with a means of inflicting damage on the opposition while they were still beyond musket range, but they seem to have been of very limited effectiveness. Manning guns of any kind called for competent gunners, and although Montrose was able to procure some light artillery from the government army defeated at Tippermuir and then conveyed those guns to Aberdeen, his artillery men made very little contribution to the Royalist victory.

Effectiveness, then as now, was a product of training, methodology and confidence. Many of the troops that faced the Royalists in battle through the campaigns of 1644–45 were men turned out from fields and workshops, hardly trained and not well-led because the overwhelming majority of the regular officers were on active service in England.

Left 56. A heavy morion helmet. Helmets like these were a little old-fashioned by the 1640s, but were still in use, particularly among pikemen. [Helmet supplied by 'Battle Orders', Surrey].
Right 57. Inside a morion. Note the thick gauge of the metal and the liner, partly there for comfort, but also to cushion blows.

58. A morion helmet with protection for the cheeks and ears.

The core of the Royalist army consisted of three Irish regiments, trained soldiers with confidence in their professional, experienced officers and with high *esprit de corps*. The Irish troops also had a powerful motivation to succeed, if they were not victorious in battle how would they ever be able to make their way home? Furthermore, if they were defeated and taken prisoner there was a very real possibility that they might be executed out-of-hand. The bitterness exhibited toward the Irish troops by Scottish society as a whole is generally portrayed as being strictly a product of Presbyterian religious bigotry, however there were other important considerations. The abortive Royalist insurrection that was attempted in April 1644 was demonstrably a miserable failure before the end of May. The belated arrival of the Irish brigade was, in the view of most Scots an attempt to resurrect a rising that had already been put down. The fact that the Irish brigade had been recruited (mainly, but not exclusively) from Roman Catholics certainly did nothing to endear them to a community that was overwhelmingly Presbyterian, but the fact that they were foreigners was probably just as significant. If Montrose had been able to import Protestant mercenaries from the Low Countries or Scandinavia they would probably not have been any more popular with the Scottish people whose goods and crops would likely suffer from the depredations of the visitors.

The chief problem facing Montrose was the sheer unpopularity of the Royalist cause in Scotland. While the King – and to some extent his Episcopalian policies – enjoyed some support in the north-east, it was insufficient to make a Royalist hinterland a realistic proposition, and the foraging (or requisitioning and looting) that the Royalists had to conduct in order to keep body and soul together did nothing to endear them to the communities through which they passed. The same applied to the government army of course, but at least there was some hope, however faint, of extracting some compensation or remission from future tax assessments from the government, whereas there was really none at all of gaining any redress from the Royalists.

4

THE APPROACH TO ABERDEEN

Aberdeen was an attractive target for Montrose for a variety of reasons. Denied entry to Dundee, he had to go somewhere, and if he was to have any chance of forming a Royalist territory that could compete with the authority of the Parliamentary government he had to secure a city that would serve as the King's capital in Scotland in the same way as Oxford provided the King's capital in England. Aberdeen was an important seaport with long-established trading links throughout Europe, but it was also in the heart of the only part of Lowland Scotland with any noticeable degree of sympathy either for the King or for Episcopalianism. Aberdeen was by far the most important town and seaport in the north-east of Scotland. In addition to the considerable international trade and the domestic industry of the town, Aberdeen was also an important academic centre, whose first university had been formally recognised in 1495 in a papal Bull from Rodrigo Borgia, Pope Alexander VI.

After the Reformation a second university, Marischal College, started accepting undergraduates in 1593; it is doubtful if any other town in Europe had such a remarkable concentration of intellectualism in relation to its population. If Montrose could secure the city he would greatly improve the general credibility of the King's cause in Scotland and simultaneously undermine the

59. Very few Highland troops fought at Aberdeen, but for those who did, the musket was the most important weapon; the sword and targe retained a significance that was as much social as military. Montrose's victories would all depend on the behaviour of conventionally armed troops, not on sword charges.

credibility of the government. Firm possession of Aberdeen would deny the government access to the north of Scotland and allow Montrose to build a secure hinterland in a prosperous agricultural area. Not only would he be able to recruit men, he would also be able to feed them.

The significance of the city was not lost on the government, and the chief military officer in the area, Lord Burleigh, was instructed to call out all the men he could muster to protect it. Burleigh was not an inspired choice; one contemporary writer went so far as to say that he was chosen 'for want of a general', but he was not entirely remiss in his labours. On 26 August he had warned the burgesses of Aberdeen that their efforts might be required in the near future to repel the rebels. Although the government in general and the local garrison – a Fife regiment in particular – were less than popular in the city, Burleigh's appeal was not ignored and the militia was embodied by a regiment of 500 men in four companies, each drawn from a quarter of the two distinct parts of the city, known as the 'Auld' and 'New' towns.

The administration of the war effort was generally in the hands of a local 'committee' comprising members of the aristocracy and gentry who had been appointed or co-opted on the grounds of local influence. The problem with such a system was that it was prone to disruption if the members did not co-operate. In seventeenth-century Aberdeenshire the most prominent groups in

60. In the seventeenth century it was not standard practice to enlist boys as drummers.

the community were the Gordons and their rivals the Forbes family. The Gordons were deeply divided because, as we have seen, the head of the house, Huntly, was committed to the Royalist cause, but his son and heir, Lord George Gordon, was staunch for the government and a member of the local war committee, which had been instrumental in countering Huntly's abortive insurrection in April 1644. Lord Gordon's efforts against his father in the spring did not convince the rest of the Aberdeenshire committee in the autumn however. His forces suffered badly from desertion due to Royalist sympathies among the rank and file, and he was marginalised by the Forbes interest. Gordon sent his younger brother Lewis (or Ludovick) to Aberdeen, possibly just as an observer, but kept the bulk of his remaining troops out of the fray. Excluding Lord Gordon from the fight against the Royalists was obviously unwise as it reduced the government army by the extent of Gordon's force. On the other hand, the Forbes' family could reasonably assume that they would be able to replace the Gordons as the dominant political force throughout the north-east of Scotland if the prestige of the Gordon family was thoroughly compromised.

Lord Burleigh and the 'committee of war' sent instructions for the embodiment of all men between the ages of sixteen and sixty liable for military service throughout the counties of Aberdeenshire, Banff, Buchan, Angus and the Mearns. The response from the areas south of Aberdeen – Angus and the Mearns – was decidedly unimpressive. Whether this was as a result of the actions of the Royalists or plain self-interest or disinterest, the recruits were not forthcoming. The majority of the men levied for service were provided by the 'retinues' of the Aberdeenshire gentry in general and the Forbes family in particular. These 'retinues' were not the feudal turnout that the name suggests. The lords and lairds of Aberdeenshire were responsible for recruiting their tenants and dependants, but also for enlisting their neighbours; they were acting not simply as local landlords, but as officers of local government with a military responsibility.

The experience and training of these retinues was undoubtedly fairly basic, but we should be wary of discounting their competence. Several retinues had been called out for varying lengths of time on a number of occasions since

61. Woollen bonnets were very widely worn by Scottish soldiers. They were knitted very large – 2 ft across – and were then shrunk to produce a very dense felted cap that is remarkably resistant to rain.

62. The majority of government regiments, both horse and foot, wore woollen uniforms of 'hodden grey'. Note the wooden mug carried by this soldier.

1637. They obviously did not necessarily consist of the same men every time each retinue was mustered, but some degree of training undoubtedly took place. The retinues would consist of both horse and foot. Since it would be grossly impractical to manage an army of perhaps as many as twenty separate formations they would have been organised into appropriate bodies of cavalry and infantry.

The retinues accounted for half or more of Burleigh's army, the rest comprised regular army units, but their combat experience was extremely limited. The Aberdeen militia regiment had been mustered several times in previous years, and had been busily drilling for a week before the battle. The behaviour of the unit during the fight would seem to indicate that their training had been fairly effective. The Fife regiment that constituted the normal garrison of the city had been raised in April 1644, so they had been in service for nearly five months by the time they first saw action. Desertion had reduced their ranks throughout the summer, and the ration strength of the unit had fallen from 700 at the end of May to only 400 when counted by the officers of the Burgh council of Aberdeen. Since the city was responsible for the sustenance of the regiment there were understandable civic objections when the regiment claimed quartering for 1,000 men. The regiment had suppli ed men for garrisons in the houses and castles of disaffected Aberdeenshire lairds and these were recalled to the colours of the regiment in time for the battle, but this only brought the unit up to 500 strong.

A large proportion of the cavalry at the disposal of Lord Burleigh was drawn form the Aberdeenshire gentry, particularly the lairds of the Forbes family. Again, many of these men would have gained some limited experience from the previous occasions on which they had been called out, but these operations had been almost exclusively minor affrays or raids on local rivals. The shortcomings of that type of experience as a platform for fighting in a general engagement against properly trained regulars would be compounded by the lack of competent cavalry leaders. There were however two troops of regular cavalry in Burleigh's army, Craigievar's and Keith's. Neither of these units was likely to have been fully trained since they had only been raised in July. Craigievar's troop seems to have been about 100 strong on 13 September, thus constituting perhaps as much as one-third of the entire government cavalry force at the battle. Keith's troop was probably somewhat weaker (assuming that Burleigh had divided his cavalry equally between his left and right flanks, as was standard practice) and may have been the unit armed with lances that was repulsed by Royalist infantry in the early stages of the action.

The government artillery would seem to have consisted of at least three pieces, since John Spalding, probably a participant in the battle, tells us that the rebels captured that number, and it must be assumed that no government artillery was saved from the action. The artillery seems to have been as effective as could be reasonably expected, producing a great deal of noise and smoke, but probably very few casualties. The same writer tells us that the Royalists also captured a considerable quantity of 'good' armour. Since the overwhelming majority of the government cavalry managed to escape the battle unharmed, this suggests that a noticeable proportion of the foot – presumably the pikemen – were equipped in the conventional style of the day. This is somewhat at variance with the received history view of Scottish armies of the Civil War period, which is that Scottish pikemen simply did not wear body armour.

Neither Lord Burleigh, nor the officers around him, seem to have given any proper consideration to attempting to really fortify the town and holding out against the Royalists. Since they have been condemned for not doing so it is worth giving some thought to why they chose to fight outside the city. There were very few Scottish towns that were ever enclosed by fortifications and even where they were, the walls were not particularly impressive. Distributing his forces around the perimeter of the city would have denied Burleigh a number of advantages that he already held over his opponent. His greater strength in cavalry would be of little value in an urban fight, he would

63. A small number of archers may have served on the right flank of the Royalist army.

surrender the initiative to Montrose by giving him a clear choice of where he would mount an attack, he would almost inevitably lose the ability to co-ordinate the efforts of his troops if they were scattered around a perimeter, the troops would not as easily be able to identify the numerical inferiority of the enemy, and troops called out from the surrounding counties might well prove to be less than dependable if they were not under close observation. Finally, men serving in the town's militia regiment might well be tempted to quietly leave their posts to protect their families and homes.

The size of the Royalist army has not been the subject of much, if any, debate. It is generally accepted that Montrose commanded approximately 1,500 infantry and about seventy cavalry against Lord Burleigh's force of 2,400 infantry and 300 cavalry. The Highland contingents that had swollen his army to perhaps as many as 3,000 at the battle of Tippermuir less than a fortnight before had mostly returned home after the murder of Lord Kilpont, but the three Irish regiments themselves comprised about 1,500 and it is difficult to believe that Montrose made no recruits at all either in the Perth area or in his march to Aberdeen via Dundee. The Burgh records of Aberdeen are quite clear that as well as the Irish troops Montrose had men from Atholl, Strathearn and 'some others, *thair adherentis*'. The writer of *Memorialls of the*

Trubles tells us that when Montrose attempted to summon the town of Dundee his force amounted to 'about 3,000 men, foot and horss, and bot aucht scoir horss of all, by baggage horss' – meaning eight score (160) horses excluding pack animals. This does not, of course, mean that Montrose had 160 at Dundee, or that even if he did, that they were still with his army when they reached Aberdeen, but it seems unlikely that absolutely all of the riding horses that he had acquired had left the army in the space of a week. Even if that were the case, the Royalist army was joined by two troops of horse before the action at Aberdeen. One of these was led by the Earl of Airlie and his sons, the other by Nathaniel Gordon, between them amounting to about seventy men. Neither of these were regular cavalry units, but, rather like their counterparts in the government army, they were probably not completely untrained. The north-east of Scotland had been the scene of numerous spats between supporters of the Crown and supporters of the government, and a certain level of competence is bound to have been acquired on all sides.

5

THE DAY OF BATTLE

MORNING

On the day before the battle the government army had retired from their position at Two Mile Cross. It is impossible to divine exactly what Burleigh had hoped to achieve by taking his army there in the first place. Having his men spend a night out in the field was unlikely to have improved their morale or their readiness for battle, and the action at Tippermuir less than a fortnight before scarcely indicated that the Royalists would be shy of an engagement.

He may have felt that taking his army into the field would have a beneficial effect in terms of morale, that some degree of 'community' feeling would be engendered by bringing the constituent parts of his army together in something like an operational setting. Having marched his troops out of the town for no immediately discernible reason, it is no easier to divine why he should have brought them back again. Seventeenth-century commanders, like all others, had to rely on information that is incomplete and they had very little opportunity to test the validity of that information before deciding

64. The bridge of Dee. Montrose had crossed the River Dee some miles upstream to avoid having to fight for this bridge. On the day of the battle he detached some troops to guard the bridge which was in his rear.

whether or not to enter battle. If his intelligence about the Royalist army was faulty – and some time after the battle one writer would be sure that Montrose had had 3,000 men under arms – he might easily conclude that he was outnumbered by an army that had already defeated one government army, and included a considerable number of fully trained regulars.

Burleigh could hardly avoid fighting; he had very definite instructions to deny the city of Aberdeen to the Royalists. He may have felt that the Two Mile Cross position offered him an advantageous site on which to meet his enemy and then had been persuaded that for whatever reason it did not. Equally, he may have expected Montrose to attack him a day or more earlier than would eventually be the case, and simply had to retire on the town in order to feed his men. Certainly there would be an advantage in having his own army take the field well-fed and rested if his opponent's force had spent a cold and hungry night on the field. Wise or otherwise, Burleigh's retreat to Aberdeen allowed Montrose to take over the position that the government army had abandoned, and his army camped for the night within a very short march of the city. Since one government army had already suffered defeat by the Royalists after drawing out of a town, it might seem rash for Burleigh to adopt the same policy, but he would find it very difficult to co-ordinate his regiments if they were distributed around the town, communication would be impeded and men from out of town might be tempted by the possibility

65. Almost all of the battlefield area has been built over long ago. The Royalists may have advanced up this slope; if so it was probably the steepest incline on the battlefield.

of conducting a spot of looting for themselves and then slipping off home, leaving the town to its fate.

11:00 A.M.

At some point during the morning of 13 September Montrose despatched a messenger, or commissioner as he was described in the records of the town, to deliver a demand for the immediate surrender of the town. The tone of the demand seems peremptory to us, but in fact was perfectly conventional by the diplomatic standards of the day. The Provost of the town convened an emergency meeting of the council and the senior officers of the army to formulate a reply, but there was no question but that they would refuse to surrender the town to Montrose. There were several reasons why they should not do so.

The arrival of an army – even a small one – would be a threat to the stability and security of the townspeople at the best of times. This particular army would have been perceived as being potentially even more disruptive than others due to the fact that they were, in the main, mercenary soldiers who were not receiving regular pay – self-evidently there was likely to be a great deal of requisitioning by the administrators of such an army and a great deal of traditional thieving by the soldiery. More crucially, there was already an army in the town. The majority of that force comprised locally enlisted men who would be more than happy to be demobilised and sent home, but there was also a regular infantry regiment stationed in Aberdeen to provide a garrison for the city and for various castles in the vicinity. Local politics provided another barrier to Montrose.

The practice of the government was to erect local committees to conduct war business of all kinds: the raising of money, the enlistment and training of troops, the supply of replacements for the armies serving in England and Ireland and the suppression of local opposition. In Aberdeenshire 'the committee' was dominated by the Forbes family. The other powerful family interest in the north-east was the Gordon family, who were split by the fact that the head of the house, Huntly, was a Royalist though his son, Lord George Gordon, was a staunch Covenanter and a member of the local committee. If the Forbes party took a leading role in the destruction of the Royalist rebellion, they would effectively marginalise the Gordon interest and confirm themselves as the dominant force in the north-east.

Whether or not there was much to discuss at the meeting, the answer was an unequivocal rejection of the Royalist demand. The commissioner, and a drummer, who had been sent with him, were given plenty to drink and were then sent on their way with the response of the council. As they were leaving the town, the drummer was shot dead, apparently by a cavalry soldier. This was certainly an outrageous act by the standards of the day, a breach of the law of arms, which has been turned into an atrocity of child murder by romantic writers ever since. As Stuart Reid points out (*Campaigns of Montrose*) it was not normal practice in the seventeenth century to employ boys as drummers. Nonetheless, it was a wanton act that infuriated Montrose, but he may have been more angry about the fact that the drummer was shot while the government army was already starting to march out of the town to deploy for battle, thus indicating that their leaders had made their decision before the arrival of the Royalist emissaries, and had therefore used the time provided by the parley to start their deployment. The letter to Montrose was written at 11 a.m., and all the contemporary writers agree that the battle commenced at that time and carried on for a space of two hours, which seems perfectly credible.

As soon as he heard the response of the town council and learned about the fate of his drummer, Montrose set his army to march quickly from Two Mile Cross toward the city. In order to prevent confusion in battle, the troops were told to take a 'rip' (handful) of oats from the fields they were marching through and stick it in their hats. Although the government army was

66. Looking down the Hardgate toward the Royalist lines.

67. Looking down the Hardgate toward Two Mile Cross.

already drawing out of the town by the time the message from the town council and the commanders of the garrison reached Montrose, the Royalists were probably not forced to deploy in front of their enemies. The government forces would have had difficulties in mustering within the bounds of the town, particularly the cavalry regiments, and then they would have to deploy from the line of march to the line of battle. The Royalists were presumably drawn up in their formations some distance away in the direction of Two Mile Cross waiting to see whether or not they were to be admitted to the city. It would seem, then, that neither side was under any pressure in the deployment phase of the battle and that both commanders were able to station their units as they saw fit, with little or no interference from the enemy.

The records of the town quite clearly locate the battle between the two areas known as Justice Mills and the Crabstane. Traditionally, the battle is assumed to have started with the two armies separated by the How Burn (or Stream), but the Burn itself seems to have made no impression whatsoever on the contemporary writers, one of whom almost certainly took part in the battle as a member of the Aberdeen militia. As a local man he would have been well aware of the existence of the How Burn, most of which is under Victorian buildings today. Where it can be seen at all, the Burn is not an enormous obstacle, but it would have been something of a barrier to units attempting to cross it in extended order and under fire. The fact that the Burn is not mentioned in any account of the action surely indicates that it was not a factor: that the main focus of the battle was some distance from the Burn and that the Royalists had crossed it before battle was joined, or else that it was so trivial a stream that it had no effect whatsoever on the advancing Royalists.

Since the battlefield has been so extensively built over, the exact location of the fighting is open to question. The salient features of the topography seem to have been that the government forces were arrayed uphill from the Royalists across the Hardgate (the main road into the town) and that the rising ground on which they deployed was to the north and east of a hill that over-looked the left flank of the enemy. To the north and east of their position lay the town itself and to the west lay open agricultural land.

In front of their main position the government commanders stationed an infantry force with a troop of lancers in support at Lower Justice Mills as a forward defence to disrupt the advance of the Royalists. A company of Royalist musketeers under Captain Mortimer of the Irish brigade drove the government infantry away from the buildings in short order, and then turned their attention to the lancers. The Royalist left-wing horse, possibly as few as thirty in number, joined the fight under Nathaniel Gordon. After a short struggle the lancers decided that discretion was the better part of valour and returned to the main line of the government army, dropping their lances as they went. From the right flank of the government main battle Lord Lewis Gordon led his minute troop of horse toward the enemy and performed a *caracole* attack. What, if anything, he hoped to achieve by this is unclear, but his actions may have encouraged Craigievar to join the battle. The occupation of Lower Justice Mill would provide the Royalists with a secure flank for the advance that they would have to make if they were to carry the fight to the enemy, so Craigievar advanced with his troop of horse to restore the situation. While he was putting this move into effect, another force, consisting of 100 horse and 400 foot made a march to the right behind the main line of the government army and out of sight of the Royalists. Had these two actions been properly co-ordinated the Royalists would have been in real danger of being rolled up from their left flank as the main body of their army was moving forward, but that was not to be. Craigievar led his cavalry headlong into one of the Irish regiments, who, instead of standing fast to receive their opponents quickly closed up into bunches to make several breaches in their line. The government horsemen passed through these gaps only to find that the Irish troops had reformed behind them and had started firing. Craigievar's unit was not destroyed by this action, because we find them operational again just a matter of weeks later, but Craigievar himself was taken prisoner and his troops left the field, taking no further part in the engagement. The reaction of the Irish regiment to Craigievar's charge could be construed as evidence that only a very small proportion of them were armed with pikes; one of the reasons proposed for Montrose's failure to carry the war into Lowland Scotland after Tippermuir is that his army did not contain enough pikemen to protect themselves from government cavalry.

The force of 100 horse and 400 foot that had assembled on the extreme right of the government line failed to give any support to their comrades, and instead stood on the hill overlooking the Royalist left flank. Nathaniel Gordon and Captain Mortimer were able to contain them there despite a marked inferiority in numbers, but were unable to force them away from the battle until they had obtained a reinforcement of another 100 musketeers from Montrose. On the left of the government line matters had progressed no better. The Fife regiment and the Aberdeen militia made no move toward the Royalists, but other troops on the left were led in two attacks by Lord Fraser and Viscount Crichton of Frendraught. Some of their force was provided by the mounted gentry of the Forbes family, but the rest of it may have been the infantry component of retinues. Forbes and Crichton took their men forward but were not supported by the cavalrymen and their attacks faltered under the disciplined fire of the Irish. According to Patrick Gordon of Ruthven the failure to secure success on the left flank was due to 'want of a generall commander, whose ordoures they should obey', but that may have been the product of local political rivalries – the gentry horsemen of Aberdeenshire, largely members of the Forbes family, being unwilling to accept the authority of Fraser and Crichton, who in turn would be too busy leading their own contingents to indulge in a chain of command dispute.

At some point, presumably before the appearance of a considerable force on his left flank, Montrose took the battle to the enemy, as he must inevitably do if he was to secure the town. For some time, an hour or more, his troops had been getting the worst of the artillery exchange. The Royalist artillery was limited to a couple of small pieces captured at Tippermuir on 1 September, and served by men with little or no experience of gunnery. The government gunners were not necessarily much more proficient, but their guns were heavier and it would be surprising if they did not have a better supply of ammunition. Casualties from the artillery exchange were probably very light, but it is unquestionably very bad for the morale of any troops to have to take fire from the enemy if they feel that they can make no useful reply, so the Royalist army made a general advance.

This was not a fast advance to contact, but rather a measured approach on the enemy to a distance suitable for conducting a firefight, probably not much more than 100 yards and quite possibly even less. Despite the force which had been sent around the right flank of the government army, the Royalists were still seriously outnumbered, and fighting their way uphill. There are a number of factors that may have contributed to the Royalist success in this, the decisive clash of the battle. One, obviously, was the superior training of the Irish troops and the confidence that they would have gained from their recent victory at Tippermuir. Two aspects of equipment differences may have had a more immediate effect. The Irish regiments seem to have had a smaller pike component than was usual in seventeenth-century armies. This would put them at a disadvantage in many circumstances, but not in a firefight; also, many of the musketeers carried flintlock muskets, which were marginally more reliable than the matchlock muskets issued to the government soldiers. The better rate of fire that regulars might be expected to achieve compared to the hastily raised local troops of the government would also contribute to the success of the Royalists, but the weight of numbers against them would still be an issue. This may have been negated by the formations employed by the two different armies. Although the drill books of the day stipulate a depth of six ranks for infantry regiments, commanders were inclined to sacrifice depth to maintain frontage. If the government units kept to six ranks, but the Royalists formed up in four ranks, that would, more than any other factor, offset the inferiority of numbers on the Royalist side. Since the Irish troops

68. Looking down Justice Mill Lane toward the Hardgate.

69. Site of a well on the right-hand side of the Hardgate looking from the government lines.

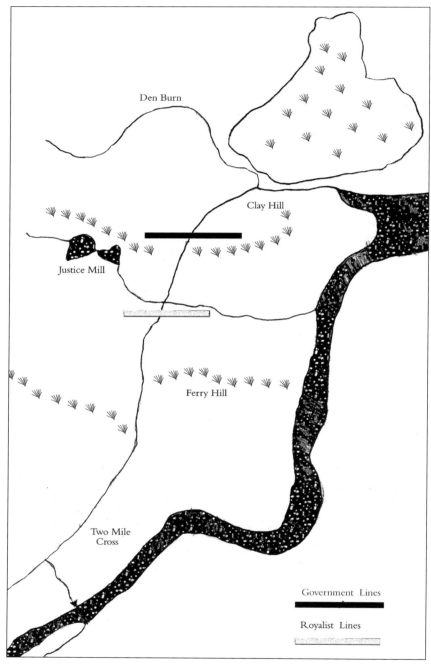

70. Map of the battlefield surrounding Aberdeen, showing the positions of both Royalist and government troops. Author's illustration.

were better trained than their opponents were, their rate of fire would not have been seriously compromised in comparison with the enemy. If, additionally, the Royalists were trained to fire by salvoes rather than the traditional rotational manner, they might actually deliver a greater number of rounds despite being much fewer in number.

The fact that the Royalists attacked, and attacked uphill, suggests that there must be some consideration that is not immediately apparent to account for their success. If both armies adopted the same formations and dressings, maintaining similar gaps between the units, the main battle of the government army, amounting to about 2,500 men must obviously have been considerably longer than the main battle of the Royalist army. Even assuming that the unit of 400 infantry and 100 cavalry sent to the hillside (overlooking the Royalist left flank) had initially been drawn up behind the main battle there would still be a large disparity. The Royalists do not seem to have had a noticeably shorter frontage than the government, therefore they deployed in fewer ranks, in a more open order, or with greater intervals between the units. This does, however, make an assumption about the battle that is not immediately substantiated by contemporary accounts – it is not necessarily the case that the two armies were neatly aligned to face one another. If the Royalists approached at an angle to the government line there would be nothing surprising about the failure of the government troops in and around Justice Mills to hold their positions. They would have the entirety of the Royalist army right on their doorstep while the rest of the government army was standing some way off.

The firefight that decided the battle seems to have continued for some time, but eventually the government line started to collapse, apparently from right to left. The force that had been detached to the right had been dispersed by the cavalry and Mortimer's musketeers. The rest of the right-hand portion of the main battle, units made up from retinues, broke up and fled. The Aberdeen militia regiment started to withdraw in an orderly fashion, but Montrose sent one of the Irish regiments after them. This may have been the only close combat of the entire battle, all the cavalry fighting may have been conducted with pistols with the exception of Craigievar's unsuccessful charge. The militia soldiers were no match for the Irish professionals in a *mêlée*, and the regiment broke and ran toward the town.

1:00 P.M.

As the militia regiment was being destroyed, their erstwhile comrades-in-arms were beating a hasty retreat. The cavalry, both regular and retinue, being better

71. The Royalist Irish regiments may have been trained to fire in salvoes rather than by rotation. The unreliability of the matchlock musket can be seen in this photograph: two have them have failed to fire.

equipped for the purpose, in the lead, along with a number of prominent members of the community who were well-known for their particularly strong Covenanting views. Only the regiment that had made the close assault on the militia entered the town, where they embarked on a spree of violence and robbery. Men of the town were stopped in the street, stripped of their clothes and then shot so that the clothes would not be torn or bloodstained. The townspeople were not even allowed to bury their dead, and the corpses lay in the streets for days. The town jail was broken open and the prisoners set at liberty, no doubt in the hope that some of them would join the Royalist army.

For the rest of the afternoon the remaining Royalist army remained 'close unbroken' on the field of battle. According to John Spalding, Montrose had promised the sack of the town to one unit in recognition of their reliable and effective service. This is by no means impossible, and, if true, it is a black mark on the reputation of one of Scotland's greatest romantic heroes. Given the level of control that Montrose was able to exert over the other units in his army at the same time it would seem unlikely that the regiment that entered the town was simply beyond his command.

As ever with battles, even those fought in our own time, the number of casualties is difficult to estimate. The author of the *True Rehearsall* gives a figure of 520 plus a further 118 members of the Burgh community, and the *Short Abridgement* claims that the government army lost 1,000 compared to just seven Royalists. The latter figure is obviously not sustainable, but the Royalist casualties certainly seem to have been insignificant, whereas the government army was destroyed as an effective force, even though all the regular units were back in action within a few weeks or months of the battle.

The pillage and rape that raged for some days after the battle throughout the city and its environs would not have been a surprising event to contemporaries. However much they might be horrified, the sack of a town, which had had the opportunity to surrender and had been captured, was a fairly ordinary occurrence in early modern war anywhere in Europe. As a general rule, a town that submitted to an approaching army would be spared the full horrors of occupation. The commander of that army would undoubtedly make heavy demands on the town for money, food, clothing and arms, but he would also at least try to keep his troops under control. If he did not, it would be that much more difficult to procure the surrender of other towns in the future. Realistically, Montrose probably would not have been able to completely restrain his troops for a number of reasons. First and foremost the bulk of his army were not local men called to the colours in an emergency who might be expected to decamp as soon as possible, but mercenaries, professional soldiers out to make a living. If Montrose was to retain their services they had to be able to make a profit in exchange for risking their necks in battle. The two central issues for which Montrose was fighting were not likely to mean a great deal to his troops. The defence of the rights of the King would be of little interest to men who had served in the army of the Irish Confederacy against that King, and the defence of the 'true reformed' Presbyterian Kirk of Scotland was hardly going to be a cause dear to the hearts of a brigade of men who were mostly – though not exclusively – Roman Catholics. Strictly speaking, as far as the majority of Irish troops were concerned, the King and Montrose were both heretics and they were engaged in a struggle against other heretics. Since there was no real ideological attraction to the Royalist cause, if the Irish brigade was going to fight at all, someone had to make it worth their while. Montrose did not have the money to pay them, so the only means of rewarding them was to allow them to help themselves to the goods and chattels of the people of Aberdeen, immediately after the battle for one regiment, and the spoil of the surrounding countryside for the rest of the army once the government troops had been dispersed.

Politically, of course, this whole episode was disastrous for the Royalist cause. The wholesale pillaging of the town and county utterly destroyed any possibility of encouraging the traditional Royalist and Episcopalian sympathies that had made the north-east of Scotland a problem area for the government in the late 1630s. With no hope of achieving a Royalist enclave from which he could develop a base to combat the Parliamentarian government, Montrose was obliged to adopt an extremely high-risk strategy. If he was to have any hope at all of rendering a useful service to his King he would have to depend entirely on combat. The drawbacks to such a policy were considerable. First and foremost he would have to be continually successful. One defeat on the battlefield would almost inevitably destroy his army and there would be no realistic possibility of recruiting another force to replace it. On the other hand consistent victory in combat would not necessarily bring him the large numbers of recruits that he would need if he was to build an army powerful enough to radically alter the military balance of power in the King's favour. As long as the government could prevent Montrose from building a hinterland with a decent seaport, the Royalist cause in Scotland would be unable to maintain dependable communications with the King's forces in England. This would obviously be a huge barrier to the import of resources to support the Scottish front even if the King could obtain the materiel and the means of transport. Success in battle would, of course, bring some benefit to Montrose's army in the way of captured weapons and ammunition, but it would not be likely to give him the means of arming a force large enough to force the government to bring the main army back to Scotland, let alone to make a meaningful, direct intervention in England. The sack of the town and county could not go on indefinitely, partly because local resources were not

72. A camp follower or a respectable member of the community of Aberdeen? A number of
women were abducted from the city and taken to the Royalist camp.

infinite, but chiefly because another government force was approaching. This is perhaps the key to understanding the campaigns of Montrose in 1644 and 1645. Superficially it would seem that the Royalists were able to strike at will, leading the government a merry dance, but in fact Montrose led his men through difficult country in terrible weather because he had no choice. However often he might be successful in battle, it was never very long before the government had put another army together to pursue him. The main-spring of his battlefield victories lay in the quality of his Irish professionals and the relative lack of skill among the government troops. The government of course had other problems to deal with apart from the Montrose rebellion. They had a large army to support in England and another in Ireland. Montrose was eventually successful in drawing Scottish troops away from the war in England, but only for a very short time. Exactly a year after the battle of Aberdeen General David Leslie, leading a strong force of cavalry from the army serving in England, overwhelmed Montrose's army at Philiphaugh. Montrose escaped, and fighting for the Royalist cause continued, but the threat to the stability of the government was over.

FURTHER READING

The relevant portions of the more important primary sources have been included as appendices at the end of this book, but there is a wealth of material available to those who wish to acquire a wider understanding of the Civil War period generally and of Scottish affairs in particular. This list of secondary sources is by no means exhaustive, merely a selection of first-rate texts chosen because they can be accessed reasonably easily through local libraries.

Montrose; For Covenant and King	Dr E. Cowan
Montrose	John Buchan
Montrose	Dr C.V. Wedgewood
The King's War	Dr C.V. Wedgewood
Scotland, James V – James VII	Prof. G.D. Donaldson
A History of the Scottish People	Dr T.C. Smout
A Regimental History of the Covenanting Armies	Dr E. Furgol
Alistair McColla and the Highland Problem	Dr D. Stevenson
The Scottish Revolution	Dr D. Stevenson
The Covenanters	Dr D. Stevenson
The English Civil War	Maurice Ashley
The Campaigns of Montrose	Stuart Reid
Scots Armies of the Civil War	Stuart Reid
Covenant, Charter and Party	(ed.) Dr T. Brotherstone
Scotland Revisited	Dr J. Wormald
Atlas of Scottish History to 1707	McNeill and McQueen
Aberdeen Council Records	(ed.) L.B. Taylor

NOTE ON APPENDICES

Although the spellings and punctuation of early modern Scots seem a little daunting, they are in fact much easier to get to grips with than one might suspect. Unsurprisingly, spelling – like English in the same period – was far from standardised, and there are several examples of spelling variations within a single document. The letter combination 'qh' should be regarded as 'wh' and the combination 'lk' as 'ch'; thus 'quhilk' becomes 'which'. The letters 'u', 'v' and 'w' are often used interchangeably, hence 'vpon' for 'upon' and 'couenant' for 'covenant'. If a particular word or phrase defies immediate comprehension, try saying the word(s) out loud in as Scottish an accent as you can muster – that will usually do the trick. Brackets appearing thus [ ] in the documents have been inserted by myself, hopefully to clarify the texts, brackets shown thus ( ) are those of the writer.

APPENDIX 1

Patrick Gordon of Ruthven.
'A Short Abridgement of Britane's Distemper'.

Montrose armie mairched neere the toune, thew Couenanting ['covenanting' or govern-ment] pairtie comes to the fieldes, and both armies drawin up in battell; the left wing of Montrose armie, consisting of threttie [thirty] horsemen, was commanded by Colonell Nathaniel Gordon and Colonnel Hay, haueing with them on foot a hunreth Irish muscatiers led by Captane Mortimer. After they had beat a partie send from the enemie to make good a passe, consisting of some gairdens and houses that lay betuixt the armies, which the Couenant had once made good, and ware seconded by a troup of lanciers; but the Irishes, at a neere distance gaue such a continuall fyre as they fand that sevice too hote for them, and therefore makes a retreat. This gaue courage to the Royalists, for they left there lances behind them; and there foule [full] retreat makes there body of hors, consis-teing of three hundreth in that wing, to send forth a stronger partie, consisteing of a hunreth horse, and with them also foure hunreth foote. Those making a compasse about befor they were perceaued [perceived], vines the syd of a hill that lay to the north of this small winge of the Royalists and yet for want of experience stayes them there, where they were so fare advanced that, if they had charged roundly forward, they had gone neere to haue carried that dayes victorie to ouerthrow Montrose whole army; for they had not only takin his canon, but the bodie of his maine battell was so farre aduanced to joyne with there enemies, as they had fallin in there reire vpon there backes directly.

But Mortimer, with his muscatyres, how soone they sawe them, makes a halt, playes vpon the lustelie; and yet at a distance, being too weake to mairch vp the hill, vntil Nathaniell Gordoune, aduertisseing the generall of the danger, gets a hunner muscatieres more to second them, and those joyneing with the few horse they hade, ascendes the hill, and routes them, and cutes all there foote in pieces.

The right wing of the Royalistes was twyce charged by the Lord Fraser, who shewed himself lyke a brawe and valiant gentleman, with whom was the Lord Crichtone, but they were repressed, not being seconded by the horsemen tymely; for the barrones of the name of Forbes, with those of Buchan, stood of [off], not for want of good will to fight, but for want of experience, not knaweing that it was there tyme to charge; and this errour came chiefly for want of a generall commander, whose ordoures they should obey.

The two full bodyes, or main battells, aduanceing to joyne, Lord Lewes Gordone, with those eighteine gentlemen he brought with him, was the first that charged with there pistoles, discharging in rankes, and retyreing in carracoll. *Craigieware fell nixt to charge with his troupe, and it seimes for emulation's sake, because this noble youth had breid himself vp in the field of Mars whilest he was abroad, would needes therefor go beyond him in chargeing through the bodie of there maine battell. But in this he did show both his own weakenes and ignorance in militarie discipline; for the Irishes, throw whom he charged, being so wll trained men as the world could afford no better, oppins there rankes receiuing him, and closes again immediately by commande of there worthie McDonald, and then on all quarters giues fyre vpon. Few or non of his troupe went backe that durst wenter with him, nor ware they many; himself being dishorsed, was takin prisoner, and ane other gentleman, brother to the tutor of Petslicoe. By this the two maine battells ware joyned, where it was disputed hard for a long space, but in end the Royalistes prevailled. In the bodie of the maine battell all the citizens and many of the garrison ware killed.*

The horsemen were so astonoshed whan they sawe Craigeiwares troupe so quickly swallowed vp within the bodie of the enemies maine battell, as they knew not where nor in what more safe posture to giue a new charge; for altho they wanted not courage to perform it. There courage was vnvsefull (haweing never beene tried in a day of battell befor). All this could the presence of a wyse general haue prevented, whose command no doubt but they wold haue followed, aither in charging in dewe tyme in a full body, strongly vnited, or in seuerall bragades, as he should see the aduantage, aideing where he sawe yeelding, or chargeing where he sawe a reserue, to maintaine and follow his point. This, and much more, belongeth to a vigillant generall, whose actiue care, whose quick and apprehensive judgement, being carefully obeyed by the whole armie, sould quickly have learned them practice.

This was the cause of there overthrow. For altho it [is] said that for want of a generall, they put it vpon my Lord Burly, yet I could neuer learne that he tooke any charge vpon him that day; and some of the best and most ingenuus amongest them confessed afterwardes there errour, finding sensiblie the great losse they had in wanteing the great aid my Lord Gordon could haue brought them, as also in there arrogant confidence that without him they were able to haue done all.

Wee may trewlie say that God, Who would haue it thus, send amongest them the spirit of diuision [division] for punishment of our sinnes; for the horsemen, being almost composed of lordes, barrones, and gentlemen of qualitie, ware all diuided in severall opiniones, for want of a head, whose opinion and order they ought to haue followed; but, being all gentlemen, and, as it ware, equalles, the generall resolution to recouer there loose, gaue way to the privat care of each ones particular sawety, which brought them all to a tymely flight, altho they stayed till they sawe the most part of the foote cute of.

All those the Prouest [Provost] send furth of citizens ware cute in pieces; the garrison ware the last that sood in the maine battell, and, being miserablie rent and torne, they, lyke bold and weell trained souldioures make there retreat in order, and too boldly resolues to march south, by crossing the Die [River Dee]; but the major general

[Montrose] perceaueing [perceiving] there design, takes furth foure hundred Irishes, and followeing them so rudly, falls in amongst them, as few or none escaped. The precedent [president senior officer] Burly was more wise in takeing flight, which he intended south, towardes the north, for, crosseing at the brigge [bridge] of Don, he went to Buchan. The Royalists loosed [lost] but seawen [seven] men, the Couenant a thousand. It was fought vpon the 13 September 1644, tualfe dayes after that of St Jhonstoune [Perth].

APPENDIX 2

JOHN SPALDING,
'MEMORIALLS OF THE TRUBLES IN SCOTLAND 1627–1645.'

The committee of Abirdein, heiring of thir troubles, convenit the Fyf regiment lying in the countrie and in Abirdene, and sendis for Livetennand Arnot, who cam. Thay send for the souldiouris lying in Auchindoun, Geight, Kelly, and Drum, and makis wp about 500 men and sendis the committee money and best geir to Dunottar.

Vpone Sonday, the 8 September, warning maid at oure Old toune kirk efter foirnone's [forenoon] sermon, that all maner of men betuixt sixty and sixteen of this parochin (except and sic as is vnder the Lord Gordouns division) to be in reddiness the morne with armes and fifteen days loan, wnder the pane of death, conforme to ane ordinans of the committee; and this ordour to be observit throw all the paroche churchis within the schirrefdomes of Kincardin, Banf, and Abirdein, bot littill obedience wes givin to thiir vntymely warningis.

In the mein tyme, the lieutennand cumis throw Angouss from Sanct Johnston [Perth], and, vpone the sext [6] of September, encampis neir to Dundy [Dundee], quhair [where] mony of the countrie people fled before his cuming, and sum regiments cam also, quhairby [whereby] the toune wes strong aneuche [enough]. Nottheles, the livetennand summondis it to rander; bot thay stood out stoutlie. Quhairvpone he liftis his camp, being now about 3,000 men, foot and horss, and bot aucht scoir horss of all, by baggage horss. He marchis fra Dundie throw the Mernis. He writes ane letter to the Erll Marschall now being in Dunotter, and inclosis within the samen ane letter written fra the king to him. He declarit his intention wes nowayis to truble the peace of his Majesties loyall subiectis, bot to be aganes [against] the traittouris of the land, enemyis to his Royall Prerogatiue; and desyrit him to ryss, concur, and assist with him his majestis livetennand, as he wold be ansuerabill vpone his awin perrell. Marschall wreit bak no ansuer, bot send his mynd be word; and syne sendis the livetenantis letter to the committee at Abirdene, schoeing his fidelitie to the countrie. Bot he lay still in Dunotter when most wes ado.

Ye haue befoir, folio, of the incuming of the schires of Banf and Abirdein. Thay war reknit about 1,500 foot and 300 trovperis, and about 400 Fyf men and vther disperst soldiouris, and both the tounes of Abirdein estimat to 500 foot. That begin to watch the brig of Die, and mak sum saif guardis and fortificatiouns to litle effect. The toun of Abirdene choosis four capitans for the four quarters thairof, viz. Patrik Leslie, younger, sone to the Provest, Alexander Lumsden, Alexander Burnet and

Thomas Melving, with other officiaris, and Major Arthur Forbes to be thair chief leider.

And thus wes oure people betuixt sixty and sixteen in both tounes to dreilling in the Lynkis and careing of armes and send their welth and committee moneyis to Dunotter to be keipit. The livetennand in the mein tyme miskenis [avoids?] the brig of Die; and, vpone Wednesday, 11 September, he crost the water at the milnes [mills] of Drum, and campit about Crathass [Crathes]; bot the livetennand him self with his gaird sovpit [supped] with the Laird of Leyis efter he had summoned him to rander his houss. He did no harme, but took sum armes and horss and promeiss of sum men. Leyis offerit him 5,000 merkis [£3,300] of money, quhilk [which] he noblie refuisit.

As he is thus lying at Crathass oure army lyis at watche all nicht in armes, and many countrie people and toune's people stall away for feir. Quhairvpone procalmationis givin out forbidding any to stur fra the camp without ordour vnder the pane of death, and whoso hapnit to aprehend or kill thame in thait flicht sould have 500 merkis [£330] for his panes, whiche bred gryte feir; yit mony did haserd and stall away fra the camp, albeit the wayis [roads] and brigis of Done and Die [the bridges over the Don and the Dee] war straitlie watchit day and night.

Vpone Wednesday, 11 September, oure army merchit out of the toun to the Tuo Myll Cross; bot vpone Thuirsday thay returnit bak to the toune at nicht. The enemy marchis doun Dee-syde, and cumis the same nicht to that same place of Tuo Myll Cross, quhair thay set doun thair camp.

Vpone Frydday, 13 September, about 11 a.m., oure army beginis to marche out of the toun. Livetennand Montroiss wreittis ane letter to the Prouest and balleis [Provost and Baillies – the town council] of Abirdein, sendis ane drummer to tovk ane parle, and ane commissioner to deleuer the letter, quhilk boor ane command and charge to rander the toune to him livetennand to his Majestie and in the Kingis name, quhairby he micht receave peciabil [peaceable] entress to vse his Majestis proclamationis and sic orderis as hwe thocht fitting, promesing assureans that no moir harme or prejudice sould be done to toun, bot [except] to tak thair intertynnement for that nicht; vtheruayis if thay wold disobey, that then he desyrit them to remove old aigit men, wemen and children out of the get [gate] and to stand to thair awin perrell.

This letter was deleuerit to the Prouest. He convenis his counsall at the Bowbrig in Alexander Findlateris house, quhair the Lord Burlly, Livetennand Arnot, Mr. James Baird, and sum otheris wes. The causit the commissioner and drummer drink hardlie, sendis ane answer; and be the way the drummer wes vnhappellie slayne Montroiss fand thair answer wes to stand out, and defend thame selffis to the vttermost. And, fnding hiis drummer, aganes the law of nationis, most inhumanelie slayne, he grew mad, and becam furious and impatient, oure army being vpone thair merche (when he wes slayne) about 11 a.m., touardis the bounds of Justice Millis. At the recept of the quhilk answer the livetennand cumis quiklie merchand fra the Tua Myll Cross to meit ws, chargeing his men to kill and pardon none.

Oure cannon begins the play. Oure trovperis persewis hardlie. The enemy schootis thair cannon also, and defendis stoutlie with muskiteires. The fight contynewis hotlie during the space of two houris. At last we tak the flight. Oure trovperis vpone horsbak wan saifflie away, except Schir Williame Forbes of Craigiwar and John Forbes of Lairgy war takin prissoneris. Thair wes litill slauchter in the fight, bot horribill wes the slauchter in the flight fleing bak to the toune, which wes oure toune's menis destruction; whairas if thay had fled and not cum neir the toune thay micht haue bein in better securitie; bot being commanded be Patrik Leslie Prouest to tak the toune thay war vndone, yit himself and the pryme couenanteris being on horsbak wan saifflie them selffis away. The livetennand followis the chaiss in ti Abirdein, his men hewing and cutting doun all maner of man they could overtak within the toune, vpone the streites, or in thair houssis, and round about the toune, as oure men wes fleing, with brode suordis [broad swords] but [without] mercy or remeid. Thir cruel Irishes, seing a man weill cled [well dressed] wold first tyr [strip] him and saif the clothis onspoylit [unspoiled], syne kill the man. We lost 3 piece of cannon with much goode armour, besydis the plundering of our toune houssis, merchand buithis [shops and warehouses], and all, whiche wes pitifull to sie. The Lord Burlly, Mr. Alexander Joffray and his sones, Mr. Robert Farquhar, Walter Cochrum, Mr. James Baird, aduocat [advocate or barrister] in Edinburgh, and diuerss vtheris Covenanteris, wan vpon horss saif away. Aluayes Montroiss follouis the cheass in to Abirdene, leaving the bodie of his army cloiss vnbroken whill his returne, except such Irishis as faucht the field. He had promesit to them the plundering of the toune for thair good seruice. Aluaies the livetennand stayit not, bot returnit bak fra Abirdene to the camp this samen Frydday at nicht, leaving the Irishis killing, robbing, and plundering of this toune at thair plesour. And nothing hard [heard] bot pitifull hovling [howling], crying, weiping, mvrning [mourning], throw all the streittis.

Thus thir Irish contynewit Frydday, Setterday, Sonday, Mononday. Sum wemen they pressit to defloir, and vther sum thay took perforce to serve thame in the camp. It was lamentabill to heir hoe thir Irishes who had gottin the spoyl of the toune did abuse the samen. The men that thay killit thay would not suffer to be bureit, but tirrit thame of thair clothis, syne left thair nakit bodeis lying aboue the ground. The wyf durst nocht cry or weip at her husbandis slauchter befoir hir eyes, nor the mother for the sone, nor the dochter [daughter] for the father, whiche, if thay war hard, then thay war presentlie slayne also.

APPENDIX 3

COMMISSIONS AS COMPANY COMMANDERS FROM THE TOWN COUNCIL

4 September 1644 The quhilk day the counsall, in respect of the approache of Irish rebells, ordanis the haill inhabitants of this burghe, both frie and unfrie★, to be put in a warlike posture, and electit Patrik Leslie★★, younger, Thomas Meluill, Alexander Lumisdaine, and Alexander Burnett of Schethokisley, to be capitanes for the four quarters of this toune in maner following, viz; the said Patrick Leslie, for the cruikit quarter, Thomas Melville, for the evin quarter, Alexander Lumisdaine for the greine quarter, and Alexander Burnett for the futtie quarter, with libertie to ilk [each] ane of the saids capitanes to chuise their awne lievetentis, ancientis, and whether inferiour officiaris; lykas, the saids capitanes compeirand personallie [appearing/serving in person], acceptit thair offices, in and vpon them, and gaive thair aithes to discharge the same fatihfullie.

13 SEPTEMBER

It is to be remembrit, but nevir without regrait, the great and heavie prejudice and loss quhilk this burghe did sustaine by the cruell and bloodie feicht and conflict, quhiche was focht in betwixt the Crabstane and the Justice Mylnes, vpon 13 September, instant, betwixt 11 a.m., befoir noone, and ane after noone, occasioned be the approaching of James, Marquis of Montroise, with thrie regimentis of Irishes and [space] of Atholl men, Strathearn men, and some others, thair adherentis, the said James Marquis of Montroise, haveing requyrit the toune to be delyverit vp to him, and haveing sent ane commissioner with ane drummer for that effect, the magistrattes and counsell haveing consulted and advysed with Robert, Lord Burghlie, James, Viscount of Frendraucht, Andro, Lord Fraser, diuerse barrones of this schyre, and with the commanders of the Fyffe Regiment, quhilk wases then in ames with the inhabitantes of this toune, and with the forsaid noblemen and dyverse ready to oppose and resist the enemies incoming, did refuise to render the toune, and dismissed the commissioner and drummer, with answer to the said demand. Bot as they were passing the Fyffe Regiment the drummer was vnhappily killed by some on or other of the horsemen of our pairtie, as was thocht, quhairvpon the feicht presentlie begane, and after tuo houres hote service or thairby, the said Fyffe regiment, with our haill tounes men and otheres of the schyre being thair for the present, overpowered by the number of the enemies, wer forced to tak the retrait, quhairn many of the Fyffe regiment wer killed. And of our tounesmen were slaine that day, Maister Mathew Lumsdene,bailie, Tomas Buck, Maister of Kirkwork, Robert Leslie, maister of hospitallis, Maisters Alexander and Robert Reidis, advocattis, Andrew and Thomas Burnettis, merchands, with many mae [more] to the number of aucht scoir [160], for the enemie entering the toune immediatlie, did kill all, old and young , whom they fand on the streittes, amongst whom were two of our touns officiaris, called Gilbert Breck and Patrick Ker. They brak vp the prison hous doore, set all the warderis and prisoneris to libertie, enterir in verie many houssis and plunderit thame, killing sic men as they fand within.

★Servile status had disappeared in Scotland long before any other European country. Free and unfree in this context refers to certain economic privileges within the town rather than any question of personal liberty.
★★ Son of the Provost or leader of the council. There is nothing new about nepotism in local authority contracting it would seem!

APPENDIX 4

LETTER FROM MONTROSE TO THE PROVOST AND BAILLIES OF ABERDEEN DEMANDING THE SURRENDER OF THE TOWN TO MONTROSE AS THE LIEUTENANT OF THE KING.

Loveing friendes,

Being heir, for the maintaining of religion and liberty and his Majesties just authority and servility thes ar, in his Majesties name to requyre yow that immediately upon the sight heirof yow render and give up your toun in the name of his Maiestie. Otherways that all old persons women and children doe come out and reteire themselfes, and that those who stayes expect no quarter.
I am

As you deserve,
Montrose.

APPENDIX 5

The response of the town council to Montrose's ultimatum.

Noble Lord,

We have receivit yours with a gentilman and a drummer qrby yor/Lo signifies to ws yt you ar for maintainance of religion liberty and his Majesties just authoritie and yt we should render our toune wtherways no quarter is except to old persones women and children, we acknawledge lykways oblige ourselfs to maintain the same quilkis yor/Lo professes and shall be most willing to spend the last drope of our blood yrin [herein]) according to the Covenant subt and sworn by us Yor/Lo/ must have us excuised yt we will not abandon [or] render our toun so lichtly, seeing we think yt we deserve no censure as being guiltie of the breache of any the afforsaidis poyntis and speciallie of yt latter articles but have beine evir knawin to be most loyall and dewtiefull subjectis to His Majestie and by gods grace sall to our lyves end stryve to continow, so, and in the meane tyme to be.

Yor/Lo/ as ye deserve

Provost and Baillies of abd.
In name of the Burghe
Abd yis 7ber 1644
At 11 a.m.

The reply of the town council exists only in a rough draft with several corrections and amendments. The council could not surrender their town even if they had wanted to due to the presence of the garrison that had been installed by the government after the Earl of Huntly's abortive rising in April 1644.

APPENDIX 6

0 = pikeman
+ = musketeer

```
00000000000000000000++++++++++++++++++++++++00000000000000000000
00000000000000000000++++++++++++++++++++++++00000000000000000000
00000000000000000000++++++++++++++++++++++++00000000000000000000
00000000000000000000++++++++++++++++++++++++00000000000000000000
00000000000000000000++++++++++++++++++++++++00000000000000000000
00000000000000000000++++++++++++++++++++++++00000000000000000000
```

In a conventionally armed regiment of infantry in the mid-seventeenth century the pikemen would generally be drawn up in the centre of the unit with the musketeers divided equally on either flank. Scottish regiments tended to have a rather higher ratio of pikes to muskets than English regiments, and would look something like this:

```
0000000000000000++++++++++++++++++++++++++++0000000000000000
0000000000000000++++++++++++++++++++++++++++0000000000000000
0000000000000000++++++++++++++++++++++++++++0000000000000000
0000000000000000++++++++++++++++++++++++++++0000000000000000
0000000000000000++++++++++++++++++++++++++++0000000000000000
0000000000000000++++++++++++++++++++++++++++0000000000000000
```

Each of these 'regiments' consists of 360 'men'. The greater amount of space required by each musketeer to operate his weapon would mean that the 'pike heavy' Scottish regiments would be likely to have a smaller frontage than 'musket heavy' English regiments. The Irish units seem to have had a much smaller pike element than their English and Scottish counterparts and therefore a wider frontage relative to numerical strength.

The internal division of regiments was into companies. The companies were not all of the same size; the Colonel's company being traditionally the largest. Each company had both pikemen and musketeers to make it a self-contained formation. The company had no tactical function. Other than when deployed to a particular task, there was no company level articulation within the regiment.

APPENDIX 7

Regiments, troops and retinues of the government army and their commanding officers:

Aberdeen regiment (militia)	Major Arthur Forbes
Auchmeddan retinue	James Baird of Auchmeddan
Balhalgady retinue	Thomas Erskine of Balhalgady
Boyne retinue	Sir Walter Ogilvie of Boyne
Boyndlie retinue	John Forbes of Boyndlie
Udny retinue	John Udny of Udny
Echt retinue	Robert Forbes of Echt
Fife regiment of foot (regular)	Lieutenant Colonel Charles Arnott
Corsindie retinue	William Forbes of Corsindie
Lord Fraser's retinue	Andrew, Lord Fraser
Craigievar's troop (regular)	Sir William Forbes of Craigievar
Frendraught retinue	James, Viscount Frendraught
Glenkindie retinue	Alexander Strachan of Glenkindie
Clachreach retinue	John Keith of Clachreach
Lord Lewis Gordon's troop of horse	
Tolquhoun retinue	Walter Forbes of Tolquhon
Alexander Keith's troop of horse (regular)	Alexander Keith
Kinmuck retinue	John Kennedy of Kinmuck
Skene retinue	James Skene of Skene
Kinnadie retinue	Patrick Strachan of Kinnadie
Largie retinue	? Forbes of Largie
Leslie retinue	John Forbes of Leslie
Monymusk retinue	Sir William Forbes of Monymusk
Muiryfold retinue	James Hay of Muiryfold
Philorth retinue	Alex Fraser of Philorth
Pitsligo retinue	Alexander Forbes, tutor of Pitsligo

The high proportion of Forbes gentry called on to supply men to the government army is a reflection of the lands held by members of the family; the duty of landlords to call out men to fight being a traditional responsibility, but it also demonstrates the extent to which the Forbes family dominated the local war committee. Not all of the men called out to serve in the retinues were necessarily either members or tenants of the family, they merely happened to live in areas for which Forbes' were responsible. The same applies to the other retinue units, and it is not impossible that for some of these lairds their area of responsibility was that of their parish rather than just their own lands.

APPENDIX 8

That no man pretend ignorance, and that everie one may know the dutie of his place, that he may do it. The Articles and Ordinances following, are to be published at the generall rendezvous in everie regiment apart, by the majors of the severall regiments, and in the presence of all the officers. The same shall afterward be openly read to every company of horse and foot, and at such times as shall be thought most convenient by the Lord General and in like manner shall be made known to so many as joyne themselves to be professed souldiers in the army. For this end, everie colonell and captaine shall provide one of these books, that hee may have it in readiness at all occasions, and every souldier shall solemnly sweare this following oath:

I, N.N., promise and sweare to be true and faithfull in this service, according to the heads sworne by me in the Solemne League and Covenant of the three kingdomes: to honour and obey my Lord Generall, and all my superiour officers and commanders, and by all meanes to hinder their dishonor and hurt; to observe carefully all the Articles of War and Camp-Discipline; never to leave the defence of this cause, nor flee from my Colours so long as I can follow them; to be ready to be watching, warding, and working, so far as I have strength; to endure and suffer all distresses, and to fight manfully to the uttermost, as I shall answer to God, and as God shall help me.

I

Kirk discipline shall be exercised, and the sick cared for in every Regiment, by the particular eldership, or kirk-session to be appointed, even as useth to be done in every parish in the time of peace and that there may be an uniformitie thorowout the whole army in all matters ecclesiastical, there shall be a generall eldership, or common ecclesiastick judiciary, made up of all the ministers of the camp, and of one elder direct from every particular regiment, who shall also judge of appellations made unto them from the particular sessions or elderships.

II

For deciding of all questions, debates and quarrellings that shall arise betwixt captains and their souldiers, or any others of the army, and for the better observing of Camp-Discipline, two courts of justice, the one higher, and the other lower, are appoynted, wherein all judges are sworn to do justice equally: the higher also to judge of appellations to be made from the lower court. And if any man shall by word or gesture shew his contempt or mis-regard, or shall fall out in boasting or braving, while the courts are sitting, hee shall be punished by death. And both these judiciatores, as well of the kirk matters, as of war, shall be subject to the Generall Assembly and Committee of Estates respective.

III

Whosoever shall wilfully or carelessly absent himselfe from morning and evening prayers, or from preaching before and after-noon on the Lord's day, or other extraordinarie times appoynted for the worship of God, when the signe uis given by sound of trumpet or drum, hee shall be censured and punished for his neglect or contempt, by penaltie, imprisonment, or other punishment, as his fault deserveth.

After the warning given, there shall be no Market, nor selling of commodities whatsoever, till the prayers or preaching be ended, upon paine of forfeiting the things so sold, and of the imprisoning of the offenders.

IV

Common and ordinary swearing and cursing, open prophaning of the Lord's day, wronging of his ministers, and other acts of that kind, shall be punished with losse of pay and imprisonment [sic], but the transgressors shall make their publike repentance in the midst of the congregation, and if they will not be reclaimed, they shall with disgrace be openly caseered and discharged, as unworthy of the meanest place in the army.

V

If any shall speak irreverently against the Kings Majestie & his authoritie, or shall presume to offer violence to his Majesties person, he shall be punished as a traytor. Hee that shall speak evil of the cause which we defend, or of the kingdomes, the Parliaments, convention of estates, or their committees in the defence therof, or shall use any words to the dishonour of the Lord Generall, he shall be punished with death.

No man shall at his own hand, without warrant of the committee, or of my Lord Generall, have, or keep intelligence with the enemy, by speech, letters, signes, or any other way, under the pain to be punished as a traytour. No man shall give over any strength, magazin, victual, &c. or make any such motion, but upon extremitie, under the sane paine. No man shall give supply, or furnish money, victuall, or any commodities to the enemy, upon pain of death.

Whosoever shall be found to do violence against the Lord Generall, his safe-guard, or safe-conduct, shall dye for it. Whosoever shall be found guiltie of carelessness and negligence in his service, although he be free of treachery and double-dealing, shall beare his owne punishment.

VI

All commanders and officers shall be carefull, both by their authority and example, that all under their charge, live in godlinesse, sobernesse, and righteousnesse. And if they themselves shall be common swearers, cursers, drunkards, or any of them at any time shall come drunke to his guard, or by quarrelling, or any other way shall commit any notable disorder in this quarter, loss of place shall be his punishment and further, according to the sentence of the court of war.

The captaines that shall be negligent in training their companies, or that shall be found to withold from their souldiers any part of their pay, shall be discharged of their place, and further censured by the court of war.

No commander or officer shall conceale dangerous and discontented humours, inclined to mutinies, or grudging at the orders given them, but shall make then knowne to the prime leaders of the army, upon the paine to be accounted guilty of mutiny.

No commander or officer shall authorize, or wittingly permit any souldier to go forthe to a single combate, under paine of death. But on the contrary, all officers shall be carefull by all meanes to part quarrellings amongst Souldiers, although they be of other regiments or companies, and shall have power to command them to prison, which if the souldiers shall disobey or resist by using any weapon, they shall die for it.

No captaine shall presume at his owne hand, without warrant of the Lord Generall, to casseer or give a passe to any enrolled souldier or officer, who hath appeared at the generall rendezvous, nor shall any commander, officer, or souldier depart without a passe, or staye behind the time appointed him in his passe: and whosoever transgresseth the one way or the other, shall be punished at the discretion of the court of war.

VII

All souldiers shall remember that it is their part to honour and obey their commanders, and therefore shall receive their commands with reverence and shall make no noise, but be silent, when the officers are commanded, or giving their directions, that they may be heard by all, and the better obeyed: he that faileth against this, shall be imprisoned.

No souldier shall leave his captaine, nor servant forsake his master, whether he abide in the army or not, but upon licence granted, and in an orderly way.

Whosoever shall presume to discredit any of the great officers of the army, by writ, word, or any other way, and be not able to make it good and whosoever shall lift his weapon against any of them shall be punished by death and whosoever shall lift his hand against any of them shall lose his hand.

No souldier, nor inferiour officer, shall quarrel with, or offer any injury to his superiour, nor refuse any duty commanded by him, upon paine of cassering, and to be further censured by the court of war. And if any presume to strike his superiour, he shall be punished with death. But if it shall happen, that any officer shall command any thing to the evident and known prejudice of the publicke, then shall he who is commanded, modestly refuse to obey, and presently give notice thereof to the Lord Generall.

If any man shall use any words or wayes, tending to mutiny or sedition, whether for demanding his pay, or upon any other cause or if any man shall be privy to such mutinous speeches or wayes and shall conceal them, both shall be punished with death.

All must shew their valour against the enemy, and not by revenging their private injuries, which upon their complaints to their superiour officers, shall be repaired to the full. And if any man presume to take his own satisfaction, or challenge a combate, he shall be imprisoned, and have his punishment decerned by the marshall court.

The Provost-Marshall must not be resisted or hindered, in apprehending or putting delinquents in prison, and all officers must assist him to this end and if any man shall resist or breake prison, he shall be censured by the court of war.

VIII

Murther is no lesse unlawfull and intolerable in the time of War, then in the time of peace, and is to be punished with death.

Whosoever shall be found to have forced any woman, whether he be commander or souldier, shall die for it without mercy. And whosoever shall be found guilty of adultery or fornication, shall be no less severely punished then in time of peace.

If any common whores shall be found following the army, if they be married women and run away from their husbands, they shall be put to death without mercy: and if they be unmarried, they shall first be married by the hangman, and thereafter by him scourged out of the army.

Theeves and robbers shall be punished with the like severity. If any shall spoile or take any parte of their goods that die in the army, or are killed in service, he shall restore the double, and be further punished at discretion. It is provided that all their goods be forth-coming, and be disposed of according to their testament and will, declared by word or writ before witnesses or if they have made no testament, to their wives, children, or nearest kindred, according to the lawes of the kingdome.

All shall live together as friends and brethren, abstaining from words of disgrace, contempt, reproach, giving of lies, and all provocation by word or gesture: He that faileth shall be imprisoned for the first fault and if he be incorrigible he shall be with shame punished, and put out of the army.

IX

All souldiers shall come to their Colours, to watch, to be exercised, or to muster, with their owne armes. And any souldier shall come with another mans armes, he shall be punished with rigour, and the lender shall lose his armes. All shall come also with compleate and tight armes in a decent manner, otherwise to be severely punished.

If any man shall sell or give in pawne his horse, his armes, or any part of the ammunition committed to him, or any instruments, as spades, shovels, pickes, used in the field, he shall for the first and second time be beaten through the quarter, and for the third time be punished as for other theft: And he that buyeth them, or taketh them to pawne, be he souldier or victualler, shall pay the double of the money, beside the want of the things bought or impawned, and be further punished at discretion.

Whosoever in a debawched and lewd manner by cards or dice, or by sloath and unexcusable neglect, shall lose his horse and armes in whole, or in part, to the hindrance of the service and whosoever shall wilfully spoile, or breake his armes, or any instrument of war committed to him, by cutting downe of trees, or any other way, he shall serve as a pioneer, till the loss be made up, and he furnished upon his owne charges.

X

No man on his march, or at his lodging, within or without the countrey upon whatsoever pretext, shall take by violence, either horse, cattell, goods, money, or any other thing less or more, but shall pay the usuall price for his meat and drinke, or be furnished in an orderly way upon count, at the sight of the comissar, according to the order given by the committee upon paine of death, without mercy.

If any man shall presume to pull downe, or set on fire any dwelling house, though a cottage, or hew downe any fruit-trees; or to waste or deface any part of the beauty of the countrey, he shall be punished most severely: according to the importance of the fault.

In marching, no man shall staye behind without leave. No man shall straggle from his troop or company. No man shall march out of his ranke, and put others out of order, under all highest paine.

XI

If any colonell of horse or foot shall keep backe his souldiers from the appointed musters, or shall lend his souldiers to make a false muster, upon triall in the court marshall, he shall be punished as a deceiver. And if any Muster-master shall use false rolls, shall have any hand in false musters, or by connivence, or any other way be tried to be accessary to them, he shall suffer the like punishment.

XII

No man shall presume to doe the smallest injury to any that bring necessaries to the leaguer, whether by stealing from them, or decieving them, or by violence in taking their horse or goods, under the paine to be accounted and punished as enemies. No victuallers shall sell rotten victuals, upon pain of imprisonment and confiscation, and further as they shall be judged to deserve.

No souldier shall provide and sell victuals, unlesse he be authorized, nor shall any that selleth victuals, keepe in his tent or hutte any souldier at unseasonable houres, and forbidden times, under paine at discretion, like as all the prices thereof shall be set downe by the Generall Commisser, and be given to the Quarter-Master of the several regiments.

XIII

No man enrolled professing himselfe or pretending to be a souldier, shall abide in the army, unlesse hee enter in some company, nor shall he that hath entred depart without licence, upon paine of death. No man having licence shall stay beyond the time appoynted for him, upon paine of the losse of his pay during the time of his absence, and further punishment at discretion. If any man in a mutinous way, shew himself discontent with the quarter assigned him, he shall be punished as a mutiner. And if any man shall stay out of his quarter, or go without shot of cannon being entrenched, but one night, without leave of his superiour officer, he shall be casseered.

All that shall be absent from the watch after the signe is given for the setting thereof, shall be severely punished. Hee that revealeth, or falsifieth the watch-word given by the officer, within the trenches, or before the Colours; he that is taken sleeping, or drunk upon his watch; hee that commeth off the watch before the time, every one of those shall bee punished with death.

Whosoever shall assemble themselves together for taking mutinous counsell, upon whatever pretext they all, whether officers or souldiers, shall suffer death.

XIV

Every man when the alarme is given, shall repaire speedily to his Colours, no man shall forsake or flee from his Colours. No man in the countrey shall rest them that flee. No man in the battell shall throw away his musket, pike, or bandilier, all under the paine of death.

Whatsoever regiment of horse or foot, having charged the enemy, shall draw back or flee before they come to strike of sword, shall answer for it before a councell of war; and whosoever officer or souldier shall be found to bee in the default, they shall be punished by death or some shamefull pinishment, as the councell of war shall find their cowardise to deserve.

XV

If it shall come to passe, that the enemy shall force us to battell, and the Lord shall give us victorie, none shall kill a yielding enemy, not save him that still pursueth upon paine of death. Neither shall there be any ransoming of persones, spoyling, pillaging, parting of the prey, or wasting and burning by fire, or disbanding from their charges, or officers, but as the Lord Generall shall give orders upon the same paine of death.

XVI

Every mans carriage shall be diligently observed, and he according to his merit rewarded or punished: And whatsoever officer or souldier shall take commanders or Colours of the enemy, or in the siege of townes shall first enter a breach, or scale the wals, and shall carry himselfe dutifully in his station, and doth his part valiantly, in skirmish or battell, shall after the laudable example of the wisest, and worthiest kingdomes and estates, have his honour and reward according to his worth and deserving, whether hereafter we have peace or war.

Matters that are cleare by the light and law of nature are presupposed things unnecessary are passed over in silence and other things may be judged by the common customes and constitutions of war, or may upon new emergents, be expressed afterward.

PICTURE LIST

1. Henry VIII by Hans Holbein. [TA CD 12, 25]
2. Brawl in St Giles, Edinburgh. [JR CD 1, 1264]
3. Engraving of Charles I. [JR CD 2, fp 228]
4. Portrait of James VI of Scotland and I of England and Anna of Denmark. [TA CD 14, 72]
5. The Solemn League and Covenant from a contemporary pamphlet. [JR CD 1, 1324]
6. Civil War soldiers' shoes and hose. Author's photograph
7. Long boots were in great demand for protection against the wet. Author's photograph
8. Boots were used as practical holsters. Author's photograph
9. James Graham, first Marquis of Montrose. [TA CD Watson, Scot., 149]
10, 11. Commanders of the Covenanting wars. [TA CD Watson Scot., 149]
12. Buff coats offered protection from the rain and sword cuts. Author's photograph
13. A thick, lined coat was vital for keeping out the cold, but soon became heavy and cumbersome in the rain. Author's photograph
14. Targes (round shields) were carried by many Highland troops and some Irish soldiers. Author's photograph
15. Scottish form of dagger known as a dirk [dirk supplied by 'Battle Orders', Surrey]. Author's photograph
16. Polearms like this partisan were very much a badge of office for senior NCOs. Author's photograph
17. A musketeer filling the individual powder charges on his bandolier. Author's photograph
18. Other than the widely worn blue bonnet, there was nothing to particularly distinguish the majority of Scottish troops from soldiers throughout Europe.
19. A few infantry troops wore red coats like this one. Author's photograph
20. This man could just as easily be a member of an Irish regiment as a Scottish one. Author's photograph
21. Prince Rupert (1619–82). [JR CD 2, fp 80]
22. The battlefield of Tippermuir. Author's photograph
23. Perth in the seventeenth century. [JR CD 1, 1372]
24. Colour bearer from a government regiment. Author's photograph
25. Government colours were based on the Saltire. Author's photograph
26. Musketeers loading. Author's photograph
27. A matchlock musket. Author's photograph
28. A flintlock musket or 'firelock'. Author's photograph

29. Musketeer attaching a length of smouldering match to his musket. Author's photograph
30. Musketeer blowing on the end of his slow match. Author's photograph
31. Musket balls were carried in pockets or pouches. Author's photograph
32. Heavy broadswords were widely used. Author's photograph. [Sword supplied by 'Battle Orders', Surrey]
33. Musketeer ramming powder and ball. Author's photograph
34. Soldiers on both sides had to make their own arrangements for their personal kit or provisions, such as this canvas roll. Author's photograph
35. Soldiers were trained to fire in rotation. Author's photograph
36. Diced hose, very fashionable among Highland men. Author's photograph
37. A wooden powder box with an ingenius spout which measures the charge. Author's photograph
38. Heavy basket hilted sword. Author's photograph
39. Carrying the pike. Author's photograph
40. A long wheel-lock horse pistol. Author's photograph
41. The wheel-lock horse pistol. Author's photograph
42. Typical cavalryman of the 1640s. [Courtesy of Rob Hill]
43. A well-equipped horse soldier. Author's photograph
44. Typical seventeenth-century cavalry. Author's photograph
45. Civil War cavalrymen's basic armour. Author's photograph
46. A well-equipped government cavalryman or dragoon. [Courtesy of Lynn Jackson]
47. Dragoons invariably fought dismounted. Author's photograph
48. Civil War cavalry. [Courtesy of Rob Hill]
49. Oliver Cromwell. [JR CD 2, fp 326]
50. Tending the horse before the man. [Courtesy of Rob Hill].
51. Typical cavalryman of the Civil War. [Courtesy of Rob Hill]
52. Although all of the cavalrymen in this picture are 'typical' of the period, no two of them carry the same kit. [Courtesy of Rob Hill]
53. A cavalryman's pot helmet. Author's photograph
54. Back and breast-plates. Author's photograph
55. The back and breast-plates were held in place by the straps over the shoulders and the leather strap around the waist. Author's photograph
56. A heavy morion helmet. [Helmet supplied by 'Battle Orders', Surrey]. Author's photograph
57. Inside a morion. Author's photograph
58. A morion helmet with protection for the cheeks and ears. Author's photograph
59. The importance of the musket for Highland troops. Author's photograph
60. In the seventeenth century it was not standard practice to enlist boys as drummers. Author's photograph
61. Woollen bonnets were very widely worn by Scottish soldiers. Author's photograph

62. The majority of government regiments wore woollen uniforms of 'hodden grey'. Author's photograph
63. A small number of archers may have served on the right flank of the Royalist army. Author's photoggraph
64. The bridge of Dee. Author's photograph
65. Almost all of the battlefield area has been built over long ago. Author's photograph
66. Looking down the Hardgate toward the Royalist lines. Author's photograph
67. Looking down the Hardgate toward Two Mile Cross. Author's photograph
68. Looking down Justice Mill Lane toward the Hardgate. Author's photograph
69. Site of a well on the right-hand side of the Hardgate looking from the government lines. Author's photograph
70. Map of the battlefield surrounding Aberdeen, showing the positions of both Royalist and government troops. Author's photograph
71. The Royalist Irish regiments may have been trained to fire in salvoes rather than by rotation. Author's photograph
72. A number of women were abducted from the city and taken to the Royalist camp. Author's photograph

INDEX

THE SECOND SCOTTISH
WARS OF INDEPENDENCE
——— 1332-1363 ———

CHRIS BROWN

TEMPUS

THE SECOND SCOTTISH WARS OF INDEPENDENCE 1332–1363
CHRIS BROWN
The least well known of Britain's medieval wars, the Second Scottish Wars of
Independence lasted for more than thirty years. The Scots were utterly
defeated in three major battles. So how did England lose the war?
176pp 67 illus. (23 col.) Paperback
£16.99/$21.99   ISBN 0 7524 2312 6

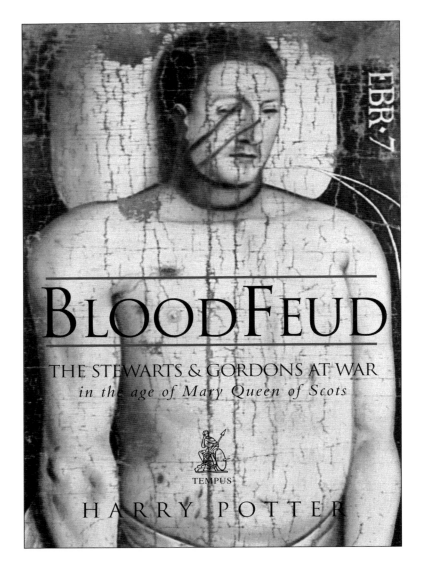

**BLOODFEUD: THE STEWARTS & GORDONS AT WAR
IN THE AGE OF MARY QUEEN OF SCOTS**

HARRY POTTER

The story of a bloody feud between warring Scottish families in the
sixteenth century.

368pp 25 illus. Paperback

£17.99/$23.99   ISBN 0 7524 2330 4

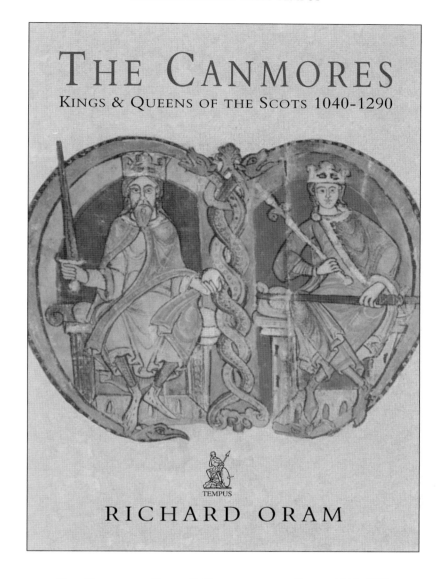

THE CANMORES: KINGS & QUEENS OF THE SCOTS 1040–1290

RICHARD ORAM

The authoritative and accessible illustrated history of the
Canmore royal family, kings and queens of the Scots from
Malcolm III (1040–93) to Alexander III (1249–86).
128pp 72 illus. Paperback
£11.99/$16.99   ISBN 0 7524 2325 8

'THE MOST ACCESSIBLE AND AUTHORITATIVE BOOK ON THE BATTLE'
FIONA WATSON, PRESENTER OF BBC TV'S HISTORY OF SCOTLAND SERIES, IN SEARCH OF SCOTLAND

THE BATTLE OF
BANNOCKBURN
—— 1314 ——

ARYEH NUSBACHER

TEMPUS

THE BATTLE OF BANNOCKBURN 1314

ARYEH NUSBACHER

'The most accessible and authoritative book on the battle.'

DR FIONA WATSON

'The first book on the Bannockburn campaign for almost a century... recommended.'

HISTORIC SCOTLAND

176pp 73 illus. (16 col.) Paperback

£12.99/$18.99   ISBN 0 7524 2326 6

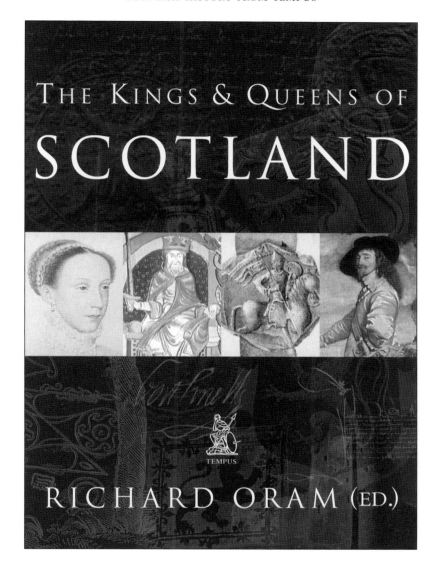

THE KINGS AND QUEENS OF SCOTLAND

RICHARD ORAM (EDITOR)

'The colourful, complex and frequently bloody story of Scottish rulers… an
exciting if rarely edifying tale, told in a clear and elegant format.'

BBC HISTORY MAGAZINE

'Remarkable.'

HISTORY TODAY

272pp 212 illus. (29 col.) Paperback

£16.99/$22.99   ISBN 0 7524 1991 9

FLODDEN 1513
NIALL BARR

'enthralling... reads as thrillingly as a novel.' *THE SCOTS MAGAZINE*

'an engrossing account of the battle... exemplary.' *BBC HISTORY MAGAZINE*

'excellent... Barr's knowledge of contemporary sources is exhaustive and
he handles them with care and confidence, shedding new light on the battle.'
THE JOURNAL OF MILITARY HISTORY

'the first modern analysis... a very readable account.' *HISTORIC SCOTLAND*

'a very considerable achievement... fascinating and convincing.' *MILITARY ILLUSTRATED*

176pp 74 illus. (23 col.) Paperback

£14.99/$24.99   ISBN 0 7524 1792 4

UK ORDERING

Simply write, stating the quantity of books required and enclosing a cheque
for the correct amount, to: Sales Department, Tempus Publishing Ltd,
The Mill, Brimscombe Port, Stroud, Glos. GL5 2QG, UK.
Alternatively, call the sales department on 01453 883300 to pay by Switch, Visa or Mastercard.

US ORDERING

Please call Arcadia Publishing, a division of Tempus Publishing, toll free on 1-888-313-2665